Happy Cake Days

To Mia

Happy Baking

xxx Wendy

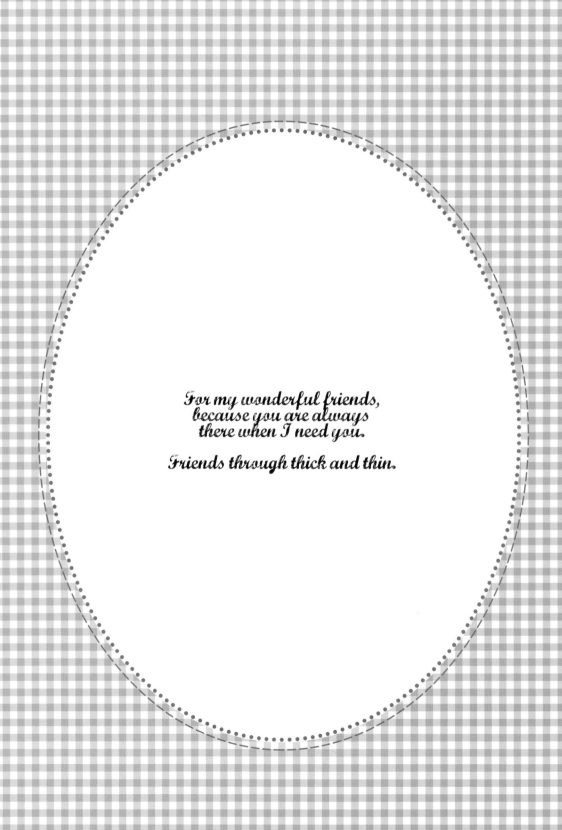

For my wonderful friends,
because you are always
there when I need you.

Friends through thick and thin.

Happy Cake Days

Decorate your own cakes to celebrate life's milestones.

Wendy Schlagwein

TERRA

© 2012 Uitgeverij Terra Lannoo B.V.
PO Box 97, 3990 DB Houten, The Netherlands
info@terralannoo.nl
www.terralannoo.nl

Text: Wendy Schlagwein
Translation: Lynn Radford, Englishproof
Photography: Maarten Brunsveld, BrunsveldFotografie.nl
Styling and design: House of Origin, Marriët Willems and Simone Kroon

ISBN 978 90 8989 547 9
NUR 441

Contents

I'm writing this a year to the day after the publication of my first book
– *Een jaar vol taart!* – was launched in The Netherlands in April 2011. And now,
exactly 12 months later, here's the follow-up, and this time in English too: *Happy Cake
Days* How time flies, and I'm overjoyed that my first book was so well received. I'm even more
overjoyed by the fact that my first book helped so many cakes to be made – my Facebook page and
inbox were inundated by photos of the most wonderful creations, not only replicas but also many
variations on my designs. And I must say that I'm really proud of all the creative ladies, and no doubt
gentlemen too, who were suitably inspired by my book to set to work themselves!

While I was still working on the first book, I realised that I was far from finished with writing. I needed to put
together another book, because I felt (and hopefully so did you...) that 12 cakes in 12 months just weren't
enough. There were still so many more excellent reasons to make a beautifully decorated cake.

In my first book *Een jaar vol taart!* (which is not yet available in English), I chose occasions that come
around annually such as Valentine's Day, Mother's Day, and such like. You can make a cake for them each year, which
is very special in itself. But there are of course plenty of other special moments in life which deserve to be celebrated
with a splendid cake – events which occur only a few times in a lifetime, or perhaps even just once.
That's how I got the idea for *Happy Cake Days*, a book full of cake designs for occasions which are real milestones in
your life, or perhaps in the lives of your nearest and dearest...after all, not everyone settles down, gets married and
has children. But I'm sure that someone close to you will be facing these life events
– maybe your sister's getting married or a friend of yours is about to become a new mum. And that
creates the perfect opportunity for you to surprise them with a special cake you made all by yourself, especially
for the special person on their special day.
For me, that is the ultimate gift and a gesture of deep affection for people you care about at special times:
giving them some little part of you, in this case a cake, that has been a real labour of love.
In this book, I also give you a peek into my life, both at work and at home since the two sides have long
merged into one. I hope that you'll not only enjoy the cake designs, but also appreciate my story behind
each one.

I've had a fantastic time putting together *Happy Cake Days* and I sincerely hope that this book
will provide you with plenty of inspiration to create some beautifully decorated cakes. I
can't wait to see the first photos of your creations appearing on my Facebook page!

Wishing you happy cake decorating,
Wendy Schlagwein

How to use this book

My aim with this book is to appeal to as
many keen cake decorators as possible. Whether
you've just baked your very first cake or it's been your
hobby for years, this book contains something for everyone:
from simple cakes for beginners to projects for experienced cake
decorators to really get their teeth into. Don't be put
off by the apparent complexity of the designs – a cake is
often easier to make than it looks.

I've gone for quality rather than quantity. This book contains
14 cake projects with detailed instructions, with the help of lots of step-
by-step photos. I take you through each stage just like I would do in a
cake class. To help you make each decorative figure, a photo shows you
four stages and the accompanying text explains the rest.

And most importantly:
Please don't think that cake decorating is something that only
other people do. Just take things slowly, and you'll be surprised
at what you can create with your very own hands!

Glossary of terms and techniques

Since the basics are generally the same, the same terms often crop up throughout this book. To avoid repeating the same explanations every time, I've provided an overview of the commonly used terms for you here.

I've also explained certain techniques in brief. It's a good idea to read this section thoroughly before you start. It will make it easier for you to understand the instructions in the rest of the book.

Materials

• **Fondant**: wherever you see this word, you can use either fondant or **marzipan**. It depends on what you prefer, both in terms of taste and ease of working. So as not to have to keep writing '**fondant** or **marzipan**', I've opted to mainly use the word 'fondant' on its own.

• **Paste** and **sugarpaste** are simply other names for fondant.

• **Colours** in the list of requirements: if colours are listed but **without weight** details, then you only need very small amounts, and you can just colour tiny balls yourself.

• **To keep the decorated cake** place the cake somewhere cool, such as the pantry or larder. It's best not to place the cake in the fridge, since the sugar layer won't like the cold and it might start to melt. The cake also tends to take on other smells from in the fridge, and a cake that tastes of French cheese or onions is not really what we had in mind. Of course, the ideal place for cakes is a separate fridge which is set to a slightly higher temperature than normal.

• **Whipped cream** does not feature often in this book.

Whipped cream fillings have to be kept refrigerated whereas cakes prefer not to be, so I try to avoid using whipped cream in the cakes.

• **Buttercream** is a type of cream made from butter and sugar. There are countless variations, but I tend to use ready-made buttercream mix. It tastes delicious, has a long shelf life, is easy to make and it freezes well. Plus it's easy to give it a different flavour.

• **Crumb-coating** is a layer of buttercream you spread on the cake to smooth the surface and help the fondant stick to the cake.

• **Recipes** are not featured in this book. Because there is an abundance of books with excellent recipes for cakes, sponges and fillings, I decided not to include any recipes in this one.

• **Mixes**: by this I mean ready-made packet mixes for sponge, butter cake and buttercream. Nowadays, packet mixes are very high quality and readily available. It's easy to add extra flavours to them yourself. I've included various mixes in a table.

• **Brushing** refers to brushing the cake layers with alcohol, fruit juice or sugar syrup. This not only improves the flavour, but it's also especially important to prevent the sponge from becoming too dry.

• **Requirements** listed for a cake are the extra things you need to make that particular cake. Naturally you also need the basic tools such as rolling pins, a knife, spatula, icing smoothers, etc. So as not to keep repeating myself, I don't list the basic tools for each cake.

• **Rolling out**: I prefer to do this on a non-stick board but you can of course also roll out on icing sugar or Crisco. I use a **smooth plastic non-stick rolling pin** but a good old pastry rolling pin is fine too. Rub your rolling pin with Crisco beforehand to prevent sticking.

• **Smoothing** the cake is done with an **icing smoother**. I find that this works better than with your hands, and you get a wonderfully smooth result.

• **Cover the cake drum**: when covering the cake drum, I calculate less fondant than needed for the entire drum since I remove the middle section that would otherwise be hidden by the cake.

• **Stacking**: I mean stacking using **dowels**.

• **Dusting**: by this I mean lightly applying powder using a dry brush. Be fairly generous with the powder to ensure a nice, even covering.

• **Glitter powders** or **glitters**: the edible versions, of course.

• **Tylose** is a powder which you can use to add strength and elasticity to your fondant. Kneading a little Tylose into your fondant will help your decorative figures to stay firm.

• **Glue**: water mixed with Tylose. Mix half a teaspoon of Tylose powder with 30 ml of water that has been boiled and allowed to cool. Stir well – the powder will not dissolve immediately and will appear lumpy at first. Allow the mixture to stand overnight and then stir well again. Keep the glue refrigerated.

• **Royal icing** is icing sugar mixed with albumen powder and water. You can use royal icing to attach the heavier decorative figures, and it's also good for piping flowers and edges.

• **Small, medium or large ball tools**: to be sure which size of ball tool I mean, it's best to look at the photo that accompanies the design.

• **Crisco** is a white vegetable fat or shortening which you can use to grease your work surface when rolling out the fondant. You can also use it to lightly grease your hands to prevent stickiness while you're modelling.

• **Cocktail sticks** are used to attach a figure's head to its body, for instance. *Please take great caution if using any inedible objects in your cake.* You can also reinforce your figures using spaghetti or sugar sticks, for example.

• **Sugar sticks** are made by kneading lots of Tylose through fondant and rolling it out into sticks. Leave them to dry thoroughly until they have hardened.

• **Marbling** is when you mix two or more colours of fondant together to create streaks. First roll out the various colours of fondant into strands. Then roll them together to make one strand, twist it and fold it double. Roll it out again to make one long strand. Repeat this process until you've achieved the desired effect. Coil the strand into a spiral and then roll it out flat to produce a marbled slab of fondant.

• **Flesh colour** differs from one person to another, of course, and you are free to make any skin tone you wish. When modelling flesh-coloured figures, I tend to add pink, brown or yellow colouring to marzipan. Because this is less matt than fondant when dry, the colour looks brighter and more lifelike.

• **The instructions for modelling the decorative figures** are quite extensive. For each figure, variously sized balls are listed in grams. With high-precision scales now being widely available, I've listed all amounts in this book from around 1 gram and upwards. Of course, not everyone has such ultra-sensitive scales in their kitchen, in which case I suggest you only weigh out the balls from 5 grams and upwards. An 8 gram ball will be larger than it appears in the illustration, so please keep an eye on the proportions in the photos. If the photo shows that the next size down is half the size of the 8 gram ball, make sure you also use a ball that is half the size. It takes some time to get a sense of the proportions, but with a bit of practice you'll soon be able to model the figures in any size you like, without even needing the instructions.

1. Mixer
2. Cake saw
3. Cake drums
4. Baking ingredients
* Ribbon
5. Rolling pin
6. Non-stick board
7. Smoother
* Dowels
8. Fondant
9. Piping bag and nozzle
10. Kitchen timer
11. Scales
12. Edible pearls
13. Food colouring
14. Whisk
15. Mixing bowl
16. Precision scales
17. Baking tins
18. Small spatula
19. Bread knife
20. Large spatula

Baking guidelines

As I've already mentioned, rather than baking the cakes from scratch, I use ready-made cake mixes. They are widely available in the shops nowadays and are of excellent quality. A number of baking guidelines are shown below. When using a mix, always follow the instructions given on the packet.

The tables below provide baking guidelines based on packet mixes from the Zeelandia and Fun-cakes brands.

Round baking tin 7.5 cm deep (3 inches)

	15 ø (6 inch)	20 ø (8 inch)	25 ø (10 inch)	30 ø (12 inch)	35 ø (14 inch)
Litres	1,3	2,2	3,5	5,2	7,4
Servings	6-8	8-12	16-20	20-25	30-35
Sponge	200 g	270 g	400 g	600 g	800 g
Water	20 ml/g	27 ml/g	40 ml/g	60 ml/g	72 ml/g
Eggs (L)	3	4	6	9	12
Baking time	30 min.	30 min.	35 min.	50 min.	60 min.
Fondant	300 g	400 g	600 g	900 g	1200 g

Source baking guidelines: www.felicitaartjes.nl and www.deleukstetaarten.nl

Flower-shaped baking tin 7.5 cm deep (3 inches)

	15 ø (6 inch)	22,5 ø (9 inch)	30 ø (12 inch)	37,5 ø (15 inch)
Litres	0,7	1,7	3,5	5
Servings	6	12-14	20-25	30-35
Sponge	130 g	270 g	430 g	660 g
Water	13 ml/g	27 ml/g	43 ml/g	66 ml/g
Eggs (L)	2	4	7	10
Baking time	30 min.	35 min.	45 min.	60 min.
Fondant	300 g	500 g	850 g	1100 g

Tip: If you can't find your baking tin listed in the tables, measure its volume by filling it with water, then compare it with the volumes shown in the tables and use the relevant quantities as given.

Tip: Fill your baking tin no more than two-thirds full with mix to prevent the cake spilling over the sides as it rises.

Wonder mould from Wilton (Engagement cake)

Litres	Aantal personen	Biscuit	Ei	Water	Baktijd	Fondant
2,5	16-18	330 g	5	33 ml	40 min.	600 g

Square baking tin 7.5 cm deep (3 inches)

	20 (8 inch)	25 (10 inch)	30 (12 inch)
Servings	12-16	20-25	30-36
Sponge	255 g	400 g	575 g
Water	25 ml/g	40 ml/g	60 ml/g
Eggs (M)	4	6	9
Baking time	35 min.	40 min.	55 min.
Fondant	600 g	800 g	1000 g

Fillings

Make the buttercream and set half of it aside to use for piping dams and for covering your cake.

Prepare the confectioners' cream as shown in the table below and mix it with the rest of the buttercream. You can also make fillings without adding confectioners' cream, but then you'll need more buttercream.

It's easy to create buttercream with a different taste by adding a flavour to it, such as vanilla essence or almond essence. You can also add strong instant coffee or espresso to create coffee-flavoured buttercream. For chocolate buttercream simply stir in melted chocolate or, an even easier method, mix with a couple of spoonfuls of hazelnut or white chocolate spread.
You can also add fruit flavour to buttercream by stirring in puréed jam – strawberry, raspberry and cherry jam are particularly suitable.

For an adults-only filling, use champagne instead of water or substitute some of the water for rum, whisky, Cointreau, Tia Maria or another liqueur of your choice. And at Easter, why not add a dash of Dutch egg-nog to your buttercream.

Tip: Square cakes require more filling than round cakes, so make a bit extra. Buttercream fillings are very suitable for freezing.

Buttercream for filling and covering (round cakes)

	15 ø (6 inch)	20 ø (8 inch)	25 ø (10 inch)	30 ø (12 inch)
Butter	125 g	185 g	250 g	325 g
Mix	50 g	75 g	100 g	130 g
Sugar	50 g	75 g	100 g	130 g
Water	100 ml	150 ml	200 ml	260 ml

Confectioners' cream (for extra-rich buttercream)

Confectioners' cream	25 g	35 g	50 g	65 g
Milk	75 ml	110 ml	150 ml	195 ml

Sufficient fondant or marzipan?

In the tables, I've listed the normal quantities. If you're still relatively inexperienced or if you want your cakes to be really nice and smooth, cover them more thickly using a bit more fondant or marzipan. I tend to roll it out rather thickly and easily end up using 100 g more fondant than indicated, but this varies from one person to another.

Rice crispies

Sometimes your cake design might call for a 3D feature. Often, it's useful if this feature is not too heavy, like the schoolhouse on the 'First day at school' cake. If made from sponge, a feature like this can be very unstable especially if, like the schoolhouse, it's taller than it is wide.

For features like this, you can also use rice crispies or other breakfast cereals which are readily available in supermarkets, and the recipe really is a piece of cake.

Melt 60 g of butter in a non-stick pan over a low heat.
Add 45 marshmallows and allow them to melt slowly into the butter.
Stir occasionally until the mixture is smooth then remove the pan from the heat.
Add 220 g of rice crispies and stir well until all the rice crispies are covered by the marshmallow mixture.

To make it into slabs or bars, pour the mixture into a large, greased ovenproof dish and smooth it using a palette knife. You can also pour it into a greased shaped tin or mould it into a 3D shape such as a football, etc.

Once it has cooled, you can cut it into the shape you want. I prefer to cover it in royal icing to smooth out any unevenness but you can use ganache or buttercream if you prefer.

The basics

Like anything else in life, you start at the very beginning. And well begun is half done, as they say.

First decide which cake you want to make. Are you going to follow one of the designs in this book, or are you going to create your own version? Will you make the cake the same size as shown, or maybe a little bigger or smaller? If you decide all of those things before you begin, you'll be well-prepared for what's to follow. If you're creating a design of your own, it can be useful to get your thoughts down on paper first. Draw the design and plan what cake sizes you'll require. Think about which types of fillings you want to use, and make a note of how much you'll need of each. Write down whether you'll be using fondant or marzipan, and the quantities and colours. Use the tables on the previous pages as a guide.

Then it's time to bake the cakes in the sizes you need, make sure that you've got the fillings ready and colour the fondant by kneading the colour through it as required (or buy ready-coloured fondant).

Baking

Get the sponges you need ready for the cake you want to decorate. If you love baking, this is your chance to use your favourite recipe, or otherwise buy a cake mix and follow the instructions on the packet.

Allow your sponges to cool thoroughly. You can easily bake them on the day before, and the sponge is easier to cut then too. You could also bake the sponges several days or even weeks in advance and freeze them. Just after thawing is the best time to slice them in half.

Tip: When colouring fondant, it's best to wear vinyl gloves since the colour can stain your hands. Knead fondant as you would knead dough: stretching and folding the coloured paste will help you to knead the colour through the dough quickly and evenly.

Filling

Before you can fill the sponges, you first need to make the fillings. Place the buttercream in piping bags. Make sure that you have everything to hand and start with a tidy work surface. Once again, to be prepared is half the victory.

✳ Slice the sponge horizontally three times using a bread knife or cake saw. You can also slice it just twice, but I personally prefer to include three layers of thinner filling than two layers of thick. This helps the cakes to retain their shape better too, as the filling doesn't tend to be pushed out to the sides by the weight. Three layers of filling can also look more appealing since you can use different sorts of fillings or colours – remember, appearance matters.

❶ Use a piping bag to pipe a vertical line of buttercream down the side of the sponge before removing the layers; this will help you to replace them correctly afterwards. Then remove the layers and brush them.

❷ Pipe a layer of buttercream onto the bottom sponge layer. Using a piping bag not only allows you to know exactly how thick the buttercream layer will be, but also ensures that it will be piped on evenly. It's much trickier with a spatula.

❸ Place the next layer back on the cake and pipe a dam around the edge to hold the jam filling in place. Add the jam as required into the space left by the dam and spread it evenly. The dam prevents moist fillings coming into contact with the cake icing, which would cause the sugarpaste to melt. Pipe a dam if you're filling the cake with whipped cream too.

Tip: Do you want an ultra-smooth cake? If so, cover it once, or even twice, more and allow it to set in the fridge each time, before finally smoothing it out with a warm palette knife.

④ Place the next sponge layer on top and pipe a layer of buttercream onto this too. Then place the final layer of sponge on top. The line of buttercream down the side should now be nice and straight, with all the individual layers properly aligned.

⑤ Apply gentle pressure to the cake. If any filling is going to ooze out, it's better to happen now than when the cake is covered. Crumb-coat the cake with a thin layer of buttercream and smooth it out. Hold the spatula upright when smoothing out the sides to make them nice and straight.

⑥ Place the cake in the fridge to allow the buttercream to set slightly, so that covering the cake will be easier and give a neater result. Remove the cake from the fridge just before you're ready to start covering it. Use a warm palette knife to smooth out any remaining unevenness.

Tip: You can give your buttercream filling an extra edge – I like to sprinkle it with chocolate or caramel, but the possibilities are endless. You could try crushed biscuits, pieces of fruit or nuts. Soft cake is delicious, but it can sometimes be a tastier – and more surprising – experience to come across a cake with a crunch.

④

⑤

⑥

Covering

Take the correct quantity of fondant in the colour required (the quantities are shown in the table). Knead the fondant until pliable before you begin rolling it out.

Tip: Only apply pressure to the rolling pin when rolling away from yourself. Roll back towards yourself without applying pressure, merely to reposition your hands. Your fondant will become much smoother this way.

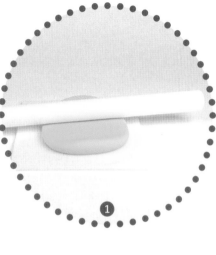

① Roll the fondant out using a smooth rolling pin on a non-stick board or another smooth work surface. If the fondant is sticking, rub it with a little Crisco or dust your work surface with a little icing sugar – but don't use too much, and make sure that the icing sugar doesn't land on top of your fondant. Note: never turn the fondant over. Instead, to keep it even, frequently rotate the fondant clockwise through 90 degrees. This will ensure you roll the fondant out evenly and in a nice circle.

✳ Check whether it is big enough by using your rolling pin to measure up and down the sides of the cake plus its diameter to see how wide the fondant needs to be rolled out. In other words, you need the diameter plus twice the height and a little bit extra to cover the cake properly. Once the fondant circle is big enough, use the smoother to even it out.

② Gently place the rolling pin onto the fondant circle and roll the fondant over it. Lifting the rolling pin, move it across onto the cake then carefully smooth the fondant over the cake as you unroll it from the rolling pin.
③ Use the smoother to even out the top surface of the cake.

Tip: If your rolling pin is too small, you can drape the fondant circle over your arm instead.

✳ Secure around the edge by pressing lightly with your hands. The edge is a cake's weak point and cracks tend to form readily. By applying light pressure to the edge now, you can prevent cracks forming later.

Tip: When filling and covering cakes, using a turntable makes everything just that little bit easier.

④ Now smooth the fondant firmly against the sides. Instead of pulling on the fondant, apply slight upward pressure against the sides – pulling it will increase the likelihood of cracks or thinness, and the top edge will be less defined. To smooth out folds or wrinkles, lift the previous part slightly and then continue to smooth it downwards again. By smoothing the fondant out in this way, you won't be left with any big wrinkles.

⑤ Apply firm pressure to the smoother along the top surface and the sides of your cake to remove any remaining unevenness from the fondant. Use the rounded edge of the smoother to smooth the lower edge of the cake into a neat finish.

⑥ Cut away the excess fondant using a knife, spatula or pizza cutter. Don't cut away too much, especially if you're not planning to add a decorative finish to the lower edge.

✱ The method is the same for square cakes, but this time make sure that the corners are nice and smooth before moving on to smoothing out the sides.

Tip: If you've got air bubbles in your fondant, you can pierce them using a needle. Better still, to avoid any risk of the needle getting lost in the cake (it doesn't bear thinking about!), use a needle tool instead.

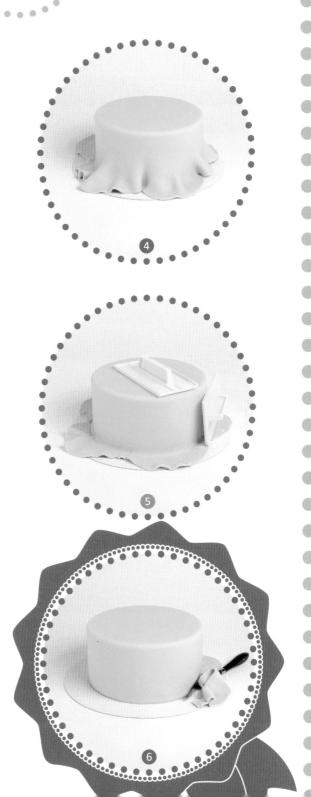

④

⑤

⑥

Covering the cake drum

Tip: For a low-budget cake base, instead of a cake drum you can use strong cardboard or MDF board which you've covered in fancy paper or a layer of foil.

To cover the cake drum, I always roll out a generous amount of fondant to make the whole process a bit easier.

However, I do find it a shame to hide all that fondant under a cake. Not only can it cause problems when cutting and serving the cake, because it makes sliding the knife underneath a little tricky, but it also means that quite a lot of fondant is 'wasted', especially in the case of a large cake drum. "Waste not, want not," as the saying goes – so I've come up with a solution.

Roll out the fondant so that the circle fits over the drum. Instead of covering the entire top surface of the drum with Tylose glue, just apply it to the outer 5 cm. Place the fondant over the drum and use a smoother to smooth it out. Lift up the drum and balance it on your hand, holding it up in the air so that you can cut away the excess fondant. Take a piece of cake card that is slightly smaller in diameter than the cake itself. Place the cardboard onto the covered drum and trace around it with your knife. Then remove the piece of fondant from the centre and roll it into a ball – you'll be amazed at how much extra fondant this gives you to use later for making the decorative figures. Stick double-sided tape around the edge of the drum and attach a nice decorative ribbon to it.

Tip: Sometimes it gives a neater finish to cover the drum at the same time as you cover the cake. While this uses the least amount of fondant, it also requires a bit more experience in covering cakes. Needless to say, this method doesn't work if you want to use a different colour of icing on the drum than on the cake.

Stacked cakes

A stacked or tiered cake is of course the ultimate cake, a cake with a real 'wow factor'. I can still clearly remember the first stacked cake I ever made: I was pretty nervous about it, and with good reason – it didn't turn out well! I didn't have access to clear instructions at the time, so I made a few beginner's mistakes. I'll spare you the details of my first attempt at stacking, but I hope that, armed with these explanations, your stacking activities will be much more successful.

The first thing to remember when making a stacked cake is that you can't simply place cakes one on top of the other, because the weight of the top cake will cause the cake below it to sag considerably. Instead, you need to support each tier from below.

Cake dowels are used to support each individual layer. I personally prefer to use Wilton plastic dowel rods – these are tubes which you can cut to length using a knife or a pipe cutter. These dowels work best if you're making large stacked cakes.

You may decide to use wooden dowels but, if so, make sure you sand the edges smooth after sawing them to length. Another option is to use thick wooden skewers. For smaller stacks, you can also use chocolate sticks, which are tasty as well as functional. Never use plastic drinking straws since they are too weak to support the cake's weight.

The number of dowels you need to place between each layer partly depends on the kind of dowels you've chosen. I've based the list below on Wilton plastic dowel rods. If you're using thin dowels, you'll probably need to insert more.

For cakes smaller than 20 cm in diameter, I've assumed you'll be using thin dowels, because using thick dowels makes relatively large holes in the cake below.

- 4 dowels beneath a 10 cm cake
- 4 dowels beneath a 15 cm cake
- 5 dowels beneath a 20 cm cake
- 6 dowels beneath a 25 cm cake
- 7 dowels beneath a 30 cm cake

Tip: The safest and most stable way to transport a stacked cake is in the car boot, on a non-slip mat. And...taking a deep breath before you drive off will offer the best chance of you – and your cake – arriving in one piece!

Stacking

Cover all the cakes as required. Starting once again at the very beginning, place the bottom layer on a firm base, such as a cake drum. You don't want the base to bend as you lift the cake up. Each cake that is subsequently stacked on the one beneath must be placed on a correctly sized cake drum, a correctly sized cake board or on strong cake cardboard. I prefer to use cardboard only for small stacks because it is much bendier and less rigid than a cake board or cake drum.

❶ Insert a dowel into the centre of the bottom layer. Mark a line on the dowel to show the height required then remove it and cut or saw to length. Cut or saw all the dowels you need for that layer to the same length.

❷ Insert one of the dowels back into the centre and space the rest around it, staying approximately 2.5 cm within the size of the cake that will be placed on top. The dowels should be level with the top of the layer of fondant.

❸ Lift up the next layer and place it onto the bottom layer, using a spatula if you wish. If you are stacking more than two layers, repeat the previous steps until your cake has reached the desired height.

To lend high stacks extra stability, you can insert a long wooden dowel through all of the layers, from the very top of the stacked cake right down to the base. That way, you know for sure that the layers will remain in place if you have to transport them. But then you need to make a hole in the base each layer is resting on beforehand which, seeing as I prefer to place each layer on a drum or board, is a bit difficult. And in theory it's not really necessary then anyhow, since the thicker dowels in combination with the cake drums form a very sturdy construction. If you're creating a six-layered cake, it's advisable to remove the top half from the bottom half for transportation and then reassemble it when you arrive.

Pretty in pink

Baby girl cake

What better way for me to start a book about
life's milestones than with the birth of a baby girl?
After all, I was one myself once – although of course
you can't make a cake to celebrate your own birth, but
that's a minor point that I'll disregard here for the sake of convenience. Since I was blessed with a wonderful son, I've never
needed to make a baby girl cake for myself either. Thankfully,
though, there have been plenty of opportunities to help friends celebrate the births of their beautiful baby girls with one of my cakes.

And now I've had the chance to create a baby girl cake especially for
this book. I decided on one which I myself would have chosen to make
if I'd had a baby girl, and it wasn't difficult to think up a design. A cake
that's pretty in pink and decorated with adorable teddy bears – I can't
imagine anything cuter and cuddlier, can you?

Just between ourselves, I admit to feeling a tinge of regret that I
hadn't discovered the joy of making cakes when my son was born,
since I think that this cute cake would look fabulous in shades of
blue too. Who knows, maybe you'll give it a go?

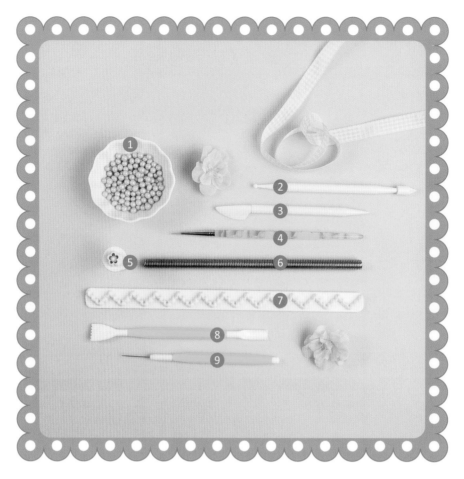

Requirements

Materials

* flower-shaped cake drum of 32.5 cm
* 2 round filled and covered cakes of 15 cm and 25 cm
* 1x cake board of 15 cm
* dowels
1 pink edible pearls
* Tylose glue
* ribbon of your choice

Fondant

* 1,100 g pale pink
* 250 g medium pink
* 250 g dark pink
* 500 g white
* 25 g black

Tools

2 small ball tool (FMM)
3 knife & scriber tool (knife) (FMM)
4 brush
5 flower blossom plunger small (PME)
6 threaded rod (stainless steel)
7 straight frill cutter no. 1 (wavy edge) (FMM)
8 scallop and comb tool (PME)
9 scriber needle tool (PME)
* alphabet set (Jem)

Method

Cover the flower-shaped cake drum with pale pink fondant. Remove the centre circle of the fondant as outlined in the basics; you'll be able to use this elsewhere on the cake. Use a needle tool to roughen the pink fondant. You can cut small nicks or draw tiny circles in it, for example – you'll see that this creates a wonderfully 'distressed' texture so that the fondant takes on the appearance of a soft, fluffy rug. Edge the drum with a pretty pink (satin) ribbon. Cover the cakes with pale pink fondant and stack them as required. This creation works best with cakes that are around 10 cm high.

For the lower cake, roll out a piece of white fondant and cut off a strip about 7 cm wide. Use a tape measure to measure the circumference of the cake and cut the fondant strip to the same length. Lay the strip down flat and carefully press the straight frill cutter into the fondant along its top edge, continuing all the way along to give the top of the strip a nice decorative edge. Roll the strip up and then fix this around the edge of the cake using a little water. Repeat this process for the smaller cake.

Use the small flower blossom plunger to make white daisies and then attach them just above the white edging, in between the peaks. Roll tiny balls of dark pink fondant and attach them in the flowers' centres. Glue a pink edible pearl at the base of each indentation on the white edging. Finish the base of each cake with the same ribbon as you used around the cake drum.

Tip: If the fondant tends to stick when you roll it up, place a layer of baking paper on it before rolling.

Tip: If you want every part of this creation to be edible, roll out a pink strip of fondant to edge the base of each cake instead, which you can decorate with dots if you wish. And if the base of your cake is nice and neat, there's no need to finish it off with ribbon at all.

Cute teddy bears

For this cake, I've made a total of 14 teddy bears in two different sizes, in medium pink, dark pink and white. Two of the bears are lying down on the cake drum. I've made the other 12 bears so that they can be placed in a variety of poses on the cake itself. This is your chance to play around: angle them so that they are slouching slightly or have their heads touching. You could place a couple of them sitting back to back, or maybe have one of them yawning or rubbing his eyes. The basic approach is the same for making each bear, so you can position them however you like. It takes a bit of practice, but it's the subtle touches in the bears' poses that really bring them to life.

To make the large bear's body, roll 20 g of pink fondant into a cone shape. Use your knife to score a line down the length of the body as a seam and make small horizontal lines as stitches. For each leg, roll 5 g of pink fondant into a carrot shape with a rounded tip. Bend the narrow end to make the paw and pinch it slightly to create a heel. Repeat this for the other leg, making sure that the paws are both the same size. Press the wider end of the legs flat at a slight angle and then attach them to the bear's lower body in the desired pose.

To make each of the arms, roll a carrot-shaped piece of 3 g of pink. Make the wrists slightly thinner and press the hands slightly flat. Cut tiny notches on the insides of the arms to allow you to bend them slightly, so that the bears won't appear so stiff. Attach the arms to the body in the desired pose. Roll 15 g of pink into a pear shape for the head and hold this in the palm of your hand with the point facing upwards to keep the back of the head round. Using your finger, flatten the area on one side of the point slightly so that the nose sticks out a bit. Use your knife to make a line over the entire length of the head, adding tiny cuts crossways on the forehead as stitches again. Use the scallop tool to draw a smile or the other end of your brush to create a yawn. For a wide-awake bear, make two tiny holes just above the nose and fix two tiny balls of black in place. Using a cocktail stick, add a twinkle to the eyes with a tiny dot of white food colouring.

To make a sleeping bear, simply attach two oval shapes of pink just above the nose and glue a tiny roll of black beneath each of them for eyelashes, so that the eyes appear closed. Roll two small pink balls for ears. Using the small ball tool, press the balls flat and attach them to each side of the bear's head. Glue a black oval onto the point to create a nose. Add tiny bows to finish the bears off.

To make the small bears, do exactly the same but use half the amount of fondant in each case. The bears lying down are also the small versions. Follow the same process, with the fatter part of the cone becoming the bear's bottom rather than its tummy. Glue a little tail on it and bend the legs slightly by cutting little notches in them, as with the arms.

Baby bootees

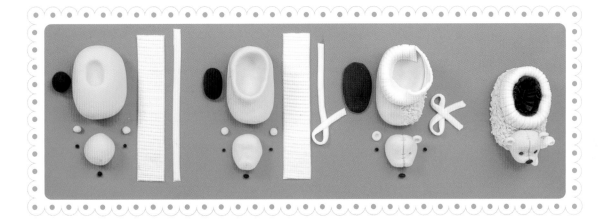

Roll out 80 g of pink fondant into a sausage shape. Make an indentation around a third of the way along and pinch all the way round to create an oval opening with raised edges. For the trim, roll out white fondant and cut off a strip measuring 3 cm by 13 cm. Create ridges with either your knife or threaded rod. Attach the strip around the stand-up edge. Shape 4 g of black into an oval and attach this into the bootee. Make some small indentations to create the effect of a padded lining around the opening for a baby's foot. Now roughen up the pink bootees as you did with the cake drum. Make an indentation at the front of the bootee ready for the bear's head. To make the bear's head, follow the instructions for making the other bears, this time using 13 g of pink. Attach the bear's head to the bootee and fix a bow under its chin.

It's a girl

Because it's always fun to include text on a cake like this, I've added some baby's building blocks. Of course, since this is a general baby girl cake, I've used the simple text 'It's a girl', but you could put the name and date of birth on them instead to give the cake a more personal touch.
For each of the building blocks, I rolled about 10 g of pink fondant into a ball, which I then squashed on one side, rotated 90 degrees and repeated until it formed a cube. I cut the letters out using the Jem alphabet set, but you could also make letters using tappits or other cutters. And if you've got a steady hand, why not try painting or piping them on?

Tip: You can make the decorative figures beforehand for extra speed and convenience.

1 year old today

Baby's first birthday cake

And so we reach the first real milestone in a baby's life: his or her first birthday. Needless to say, I'm not going to cover every birthday in this book – but a child's (or grandchild's) first birthday is a particularly special occasion.

I think that a baby's first birthday is mostly a time to reflect, to think back over the past year and remember the day this little miracle was born. A time that you're mainly amazed at how the time has flown by, and how quickly that helpless little creature has turned into this mini-person, a bundle of energy and curiosity, who might even be sticking their fingers in the cake right now.

For me, the first birthday is also a reminder of how a child is growing and changing. Maybe baby's already taken his or her first steps, the gurgles are starting to sound vaguely recognisable, and there's a hint of a naughty streak emerging.

That prompted me to make a slightly mischievous children's cake, because after baby's first steps comes baby throwing things, baby scribbling on the walls and baby tugging on the tablecloth, to name but a few! The birthday boy or girl's parents will have their hands full from now on. But remember above all to enjoy that tiny face filled with wonder and astonishment at all the things waiting to be discovered in this big wide world of ours.

Personally, I'll never forget the look of pride on my son's face as he admired the first 'masterpiece' he'd created on my living room wall while my back was turned. It was impossible to stay angry with him for long.

I really enjoyed making this cake, decorated with children at play, and it was fun to stack the layers differently for a change – it was a bit like playtime for me too! I wonder what this design will inspire you to create.

Requirements
Materials
* square cake drum of 27.5 cm
* 4 square filled and covered cakes of 20 cm 12.5 cm, 10 cm and 6 cm
* a round cake of 6 cm in diameter by 7 cm high
* cake cardboard for underneath each layer
* dowels
* a 7.5 cm high polystyrene Easter egg
* Tylose glue
❹ orange edible pearls
❺ pink dust
⑮ black florist's wire
⑯ posy picks
* ribbon of your choice

Fondant
* 1,200 g white
* 300 g brown
* 100 g red/blue/yellow/green
* a little bit of black
* 30 g flesh-coloured marzipan

Tools
❶ round cutter set (Städter)
❷ sugarcraft gun, using disc with smallest hole
❸ round & wavy edge cutter set/4 (PME) knife scriber
❻ triangular cutters (lines of flags from Cakes by Bien)
❼ brush
❽ scallop and comb tool (PME)
❾ scriber needle tool (PME)
❿ tool (knife) (FMM)
⑪ small ball tool (FMM)
⑫ wood grain impression mat (FMM)
⑬ closed scallop serrated crimper 3/4 (PME)
⑭ strip cutter no. 2 and 4 (Jem)

Method

For this cake, I've baked and filled the bottom layer to be slightly higher than the smaller cakes which are placed on top of it. The bottom layer is 10 cm high and all the other cakes are 7 cm high, to prevent the smaller cakes being much higher than they are wide. The smaller a cake is, the harder it is to cover, so by baking the cakes slightly less tall, you make things a bit easier for yourself. Cover all four cakes with white fondant.

Place the largest cake on the cake drum. Roll out some brown fondant and use the impression mat to create a wood grain effect. Use strip cutter no. 4 to cut it into floorboards. Lay the floorboards to cover the drum, right up to the edge of the cake. Lay several short floorboards end to end to create the effect of a real wooden floor, including joins. Attach a pretty ribbon around the edge of the drum to finish it off.

Cover the polystyrene egg with yellow fondant and draw a smiley face on it to make a balloon. Glue a little black ball at the pointed end of the egg. Make a small hole in a cone of yellow and attach this to the black ball to create the balloon's opening.

Decide how best to place the two smallest cakes on top of the bottom layer so that you leave a corner free for the balloon. Insert some dowels under both of the cakes to support their weight, then place them on the bottom layer. Put a dowel in the bottom cake where the balloon will go. Then place the 12.5 cm cake on top. Lay some more floorboards on the top layer, leaving the edges uneven for extra playfulness. Lay some floorboards on the layer below too.

Cover the round cake that will be the table with the white fondant – not too neatly, so that it looks like a tablecloth. You can use a large round cutter to remove the surplus fondant in one go. Press the fondant slightly inwards in places. Don't forget to insert dowels in the top layer to support this cake. Roll out green fondant and cut out a square measuring 10 cm by 10 cm and secure this cloth onto the table at an angle so that looks like the girl has given it a good tug.

Tip: When covering square cakes, it's important that the cakes are allowed to cool properly after crumb-coating before covering them, to avoid damaging the corners. First cover the corners and smooth them downwards, then smooth out the sides.

37

Girl

To make each leg, roll a sausage from 2.5 g of flesh-coloured fondant. Roll one end into a point. For the white socks, roll two sausage shapes of 1.5 g each. Make an opening in the socks and insert the legs. Bend the socks halfway along and pinch them to make heels. Make sure that both feet are the same size. Make a few marks on the socks to create a fabric effect. Stick the knees together with the toes pointing downwards.

For the dress, roll 22 g of blue fondant into a sausage shape. Make an indentation at one end and pinch around the edges to extend them. Roll with your finger to create a waist and attach the dress onto the legs, angled slightly to the back so that the dress overlaps the knees. Press the fondant around the knees slightly and make some folds in the dress. Hollow out the top of the dress and fill this with a sausage from 1 g of white. Add a bit of white to create the collar and insert a cocktail stick.

To make each arm, roll a sausage from 2.5 g of white. Glue a tiny ball of white to one end for the cuffs and make a hole in it for the hand. If you want to bend the arms, make two small cuts on one side for ease. For the hands, take two small rolls of flesh-coloured marzipan and flatten them slightly. Pinch to create a thumb just below the wrist. Extend the piece for the fingers and flatten it a bit more. Make three grooves for the fingers and bend the hands into shape. Flatten the wrists slightly by rolling with your finger, and glue the hands into the sleeves. Attach the sleeves to the dress and glue the hands onto the tablecloth.

Make the girl's face using 6.5 g of flesh-coloured marzipan. Gently flatten half the face while rolling to create contours. Use the small ball tool to create two eye sockets, which you can fill with two tiny balls of white. Flatten two tiny balls of blue and attach them to the lower half of the eyeballs, then glue on black pupils. Finish off with a dot of white food colouring to add a twinkle. Use the scallop tool to create a smiley mouth and make a hole for the nose. Roll a tiny cone for the nose and glue it in the hole. Use dust to create rosy cheeks.

For the hair, take a ball of 4.5 g of brown fondant. Use a ball tool to hollow it out. Pinch it flat all the way round to create a kind of a hood. Glue this onto the head, around the face. Use a knife to create a centre parting and score some lines as hair. Secure the head on the body using the cocktail stick. Attach two tiny balls of blue, one on each side of the head, and make a sizeable hole in them. Cut a ball of 1 g of brown in half and roll two sausages. Score some lines as shown to create plaits. Use glue to secure the plaits in the holes.

Baby's first steps

Make a long sausage from 16 g of blue fondant and fold it in half. Flatten the bottom ends. Make some small cuts at the back of the knees and bend the legs slightly. Roll two white balls for the socks and attach these to the bottom of the legs. For the pullover, roll a sausage from 15 g of yellow fondant. Make an indentation at one end and pinch to extend the edges, creating a hollow. Attach the trousers.

To make each arm, roll a sausage from 3.5 g of yellow. Glue a tiny ball of blue at one end as the cuffs and make a hole in it for the hand. If you want to bend the arms, make two small cuts on one side for ease. For the hands, take two small rolls of dark-flesh-coloured marzipan and flatten them slightly. Pinch to create a thumb just below the wrist. Extend the piece for the fingers and flatten it a bit more. Make three grooves for the fingers and bend the hands into shape. Flatten the wrists slightly and secure the hands in the sleeves.

Make the boy's face using 6.5 g of dark-flesh-coloured marzipan. Gently flatten half the face while rolling to create contours. Use the small ball tool to create two eye sockets, which you can fill with two tiny balls of white. Flatten two tiny balls of blue and attach them to the lower half of the eyeballs, then glue on black pupils. Finish off with a dot of white food colouring to add a twinkle.

Use the scallop tool to create a smiley mouth and hollow out the mouth slightly. Fill the hole with some white for teeth. Make a hole for the nose. Roll a tiny cone for the nose and glue it in the hole. For the ears, use a mini-ball tool to make two tiny balls, one on each side of the face, and press these back slightly a third of the way up.

Glue pieces of black fondant onto the head and use your needle tool to create the effect of a mass of curls on the boy's head. Attach the neck and head to the body as above and then fix him in place on the cake.

Scribbling on the walls

For the kneeling boy, use the same amounts of fondant as for the standing boy. Make his trousers as described above, but this time bend his knees right back. Make the red shoes as described for the socks, but now secure a flat oval of white underneath each one and score lines on them. Make the red pullover and the hands as described for the yellow pullover, but this time make the neck slightly thicker as a turtleneck and don't make the cuffs.

Note: When I mention flesh-coloured fondant, you can of course make it in any skin tone you choose. I've used light and dark flesh colours here to give you an idea. Feel free to experiment.

The method is the same for his face, too, or maybe you prefer to make him with closed eyes by simply drawing lines for his eyes using a food decorating pen.

For the cap, slightly flatten a ball of 4.5 g of blue. Score lines into it and glue a tiny ball in its centre. Cut out a small circle and then cut the edge off it to make the cap's visor. Roll out a thin strip of yellow and score lines into it for the hair.

Cut off the top third of the head and attach the hair to the back, up against the edge. Glue the visor on top, and then the cap on top of that.

Mini-birthday cake

Knead some Tylose through some blue fondant. Roll this out and cut out a circle of 5.5 cm in diameter. Allow this to dry. For the cakes, roll a thick layer of white fondant out flat to a thickness of 2.5 cm. From this, cut out a circle of 5 cm in diameter and a circle of 3.5 cm in diameter. Use a crimper to create a nice decorative finish along the lower edges. Use the wavy edge cutters to cut out two red frills, one of 5 cm and one of 7 cm. Attach these to the cakes, then secure the two cakes together and attach them onto the blue circle. Make a swirl of whipped cream on the cake by winding a strand of white and either insert a miniature candle into the top or make a tiny candle from some leftover fondant. Decorate the cake with some orange edible pearls as a final touch.

Tip: If the arms are a bit droopy, use small pieces of sponge for extra support.

Tip: You can make the decorative figures beforehand for extra speed and convenience

Tip: If you're struggling to squeeze the fondant through the smallest-holed disc on your sugarcraft gun, knead a little vegetable shortening such as Crisco through the fondant or heat it briefly in the microwave.

Cut a long cocktail stick or wooden skewer to 8 cm in length. Insert the stick vertically into the table until you reach the cardboard. Now attach the mini-birthday cake at an angle, so that it seems like it will topple off the table at any moment.

The finishing touches

Using the disc with the smallest hole in the sugarcraft gun, squeeze out thin strands of black fondant as bunting lines which you can attach around the cake layers as desired. Stick a bow on each corner. Cut flags in various colours using the triangular cutter and glue these onto the black fondant strands. Attach a black strand to the big yellow balloon too.

Make small balloons by rolling cones of approximately 5 g. Attach a tiny ball of black and then make the balloon's mouth. Stick the balloons on pieces of black florist's wire and insert them into a dummy while they dry. It's best to bend the wire into a hook shape first before you insert it into the balloon, to prevent the balloon sliding down over the point.

Make some presents by shaping fondant of any colour into differently sized cubes. Using the strip cutter no. 2, cut out some strips of white fondant to decorate the presents, and add a bow here and there.

Use the strip cutter no. 2 to cut strips in different colours. Wrap them around a cocktail stick and then remove the stick to create coils. Allow them to dry thoroughly. Decorate the cake with the gifts and coils and, to finish off, attach all the balloons where you want them. If you wish to push the wires into the cake, you can use posy picks.

Backpack on and off they go

First day at school

And so we come to another very important day. For most children, it's the first milestone that they themselves actually experience as a big step: their very first day at school.

Some children see it as a great adventure and can't wait to start school, while for others the tension mounts as the day draws nearer, and some are simply adamant that they don't want to go at all. Funnily enough, it's usually Mum who's the most nervous of all. However you approach the day, it should be a proud and very special moment, once again serving to remind you how quickly they grow up.

For this first day at school, I've made a girl standing on the steps to her new school. In the playground, I've designed a modern yet cute take on the rocking horse. They're mounted on wire springs so they really wobble. Just don't go too wild – after all, it's still a real cake!

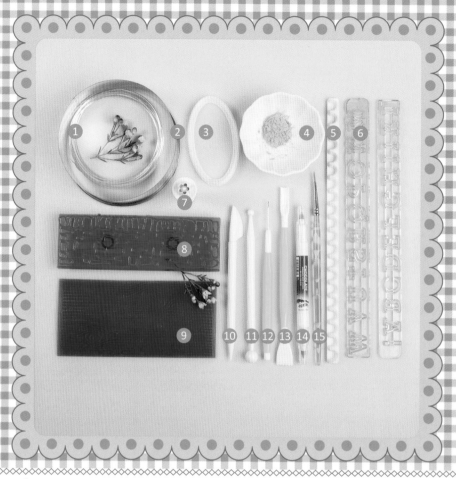

Requirements
Materials
* ✱ round cake drum of 27.5 cm
* ✱ 1 round filled and covered cake of 20 cm
* ✱ sponge or rice crispies slabs
* ❶ strong florist's wire
* ❹ pink dust
* ⑭ brown food decorating pen
* ✱ Tylose glue
* ✱ ribbon of your choice

Fondant
* ✱ 600 g green
* ✱ 250 g white
* ✱ 350 g grey
* ✱ blue/pink/black/brown/ yellow
* ✱ flesh-coloured marzipan

Tools
* ❷ round cutter 10 cm
* ❸ oval cutter
* ❺ straight frill cutter no. 3 (arched edge) (FMM)
* ❻ Alphabet & Numbers tap-pits Upper Case (FMM)
* ❼ flower blossom plunger small (PME)
* ❽ cobblestone wall cutter (Jem)
* ❾ impression mat wood grain (FMM)
* ⑩ knife scriber tool (knife) (FMM)
* ⑪ small ball tool (FMM)
* ⑫ scriber needle tool (PME)
* ⑬ scallop and comb tool (PME)
* ⑮ brush

Method

Place the filled and covered cake 2 cm from one edge of the cake drum. Measure the cake's height and divide it by three. Slice your cake or rice crispies slab into pieces of this thickness and then cut two circles using the 10 cm round cutter. Cut a third off one of the circles, glue this on top of the remaining two-thirds and then these onto the other circle to create steps. Cut the back off straight, making the steps no deeper than the space available on the drum. Cut the sides off straight and secure the steps up against the side of the cake, then cover them with buttercream or royal icing. Fill the deep gaps on both sides of the steps with bits of cake, rice crispies, fondant or marzipan to create a bumpy effect. Cover the cake with green fondant, including the steps and cake drum at the same time. Remove the excess fondant from the drum and finish off by attaching a nice ribbon around the drum.

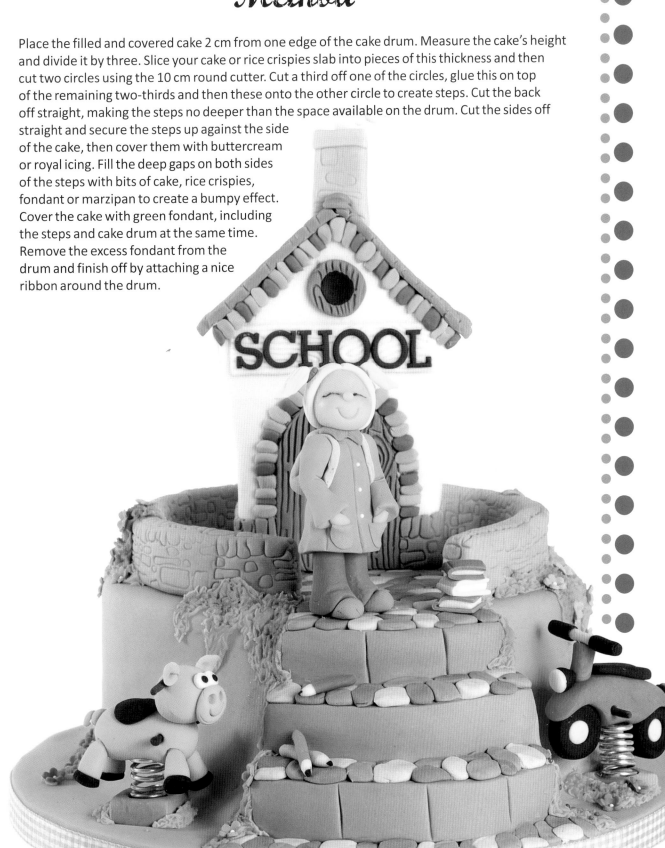

Cobblestones and wall

To make the school playground, place a piece of cake cardboard measuring 15 cm in diameter on top of the cake and trace around it gently using a needle tool to draw a circle on the cake.

Cut out strips of grey fondant to fit the front edge of the steps and glue them on. You can score lines into them if you wish. Take three pieces of 50 g fondant, in light grey, grey and brown. Roll them into thin sausages and slice them into small pieces, which you then flatten. Glue them onto the steps, alternating the colours, to look like cobblestones. Fill the circle from the top of the steps to create the school playground.

Roll 200 g of grey fondant into a sausage that is just long enough to wrap around the edge of the playground as far as the cobblestones. Press the top edge of the cobblestone wall cutter lightly against this sausage. Turn the roll on its side and flatten it. Now press the cutter firmly into the wall, repeating this until the pattern is embossed in the full length of the wall. Turn it over and repeat for the other side of the wall. Set the wall upright again and flatten the ends slightly with the patterned cutter. You can now fix the wall in place around the edge of the playground.

Schoolhouse

Cut the schoolhouse out of cake or rice crispies using the template on page 131.
Cover the schoolhouse with buttercream or royal icing. Use the templates to cut out the white fondant pieces too, but cut these generously. Cover all four sides of the house. Cut the two roof sections from grey fondant and use the straight frill cutter no. 3 to add a wavy edge and a roof-tile pattern. Use this to cut off the lower edge too, then secure the two parts on the schoolhouse.

Use the template to cut the chimney from a thick piece of rolled white fondant and emboss the brick pattern. Glue a square of black on top and finish the edge off with a strip of white. Fix the chimney to the schoolhouse. Finish off the ridge of the roof with tiny balls of grey that you have flattened. Make a wisp of smoke and attach it in the chimney using a cocktail stick.

Roll out brown fondant and emboss it with the pattern from the wood grain mat. Cut out a door using an oval cutter and slice the bottom off straight. Glue the door to the front of the schoolhouse. Cut a small circle for the window too. Cut another smaller circle from it and glue a small circle of black behind it, then attach it beneath the point of the gable. Cut out a strip of grey and emboss it with the brick pattern. Attach this strip from one side of the door, all the way around the base of the schoolhouse until you reach the other side of the door.

Roll three strands – pink, blue and green – and flatten them slightly. Slice them into tiny pieces and attach them, alternating the colours, around the door and the edge of the gable. Use the alphabet tappits to cut the word 'SCHOOL' out of black fondant. Cut a rectangle of white and glue the letters onto it, then attach the sign to the schoolhouse.

Tip: You can also make a dummy schoolhouse by using a warm knife to cut the shapes out of polystyrene. That way, you can keep it for posterity.

Tip: You can change the schoolgirl into a schoolboy simply by changing the colour and style of the hair

Schoolgirl

For each leg, use a carrot-shaped piece of 4 g of blue fondant. Flatten the wide end to form the bottom of the trouser leg. Press the trouser legs upwards slightly at the front for the shoes. Roll two pink cones for the shoes and secure them under the trouser legs. Insert cocktail sticks into the legs and stick them into a dummy for now. For the jacket, roll a thick sausage from 23 g of pink fondant. Make an indentation at one end, pinching around the edges to create a hollow. Score a line down the front and make tiny holes for the buttons, filling them with tiny balls of white fondant. Fix the jacket onto the trousers using the cocktail sticks and glue. Attach two green strands from the shoulders and under the arms as backpack straps. For the collar, flatten a tiny ball of pink and cut a tiny wedge out of it, then attach the collar to the jacket. For the backpack, make a long green cone from 5 g. Flatten the wide end from below. Roll and flatten the narrow end and fold it down as a flap. Score tiny lines into the sides of the backpack. Attach a blue button onto the flap.

For each arm, roll a pink sausage from 3 g. Flatten one end and make a hole in it. To bend the arms, roll the sausage slightly thinner in the middle and make two tiny cuts on one side before bending. Attach the arms against the jacket with the lower edges angled forwards slightly. For the hands, take two tiny flesh-coloured rolls of marzipan. Flatten them slightly and glue them in the sleeves and against the jacket. Flatten a pink oval and slice it in half, then attach both halves to the jacket as pockets, with the flat edge at the top and just over the hands.

Model the schoolgirl's face from 6 g of flesh-coloured marzipan. Gently flatten half the face while rolling to create contours. Draw two arches with a brown food decorating pen. Use the scallop tool to create a smile. Make rosy cheeks by dusting with a little bit of pink. Make a hole where the nose will go, then fill it with a tiny cone of flesh-coloured fondant.

For the hair, make a ball from 4 g of light yellow fondant. Use a ball tool to make an indentation. Pinch this flat all the way around to create a kind of a cap and then attach it to the head. Use a knife to score a centre parting and make some lines as hair. Stick the head to the body using a cocktail stick. Glue a tiny ball of blue to both sides of the head and make a hole in each one, not

Tip: You can make the decorative figures beforehand for extra speed and convenience.

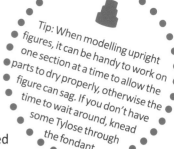
Tip: When modelling upright figures, it can be handy to work on one section at a time to allow the parts to dry properly, otherwise the figure can sag. If you don't have time to wait around, knead some Tylose through the fondant.

too small. Slice a 1 g ball of yellow in half and make each half into a pointed cone to create pigtails. Score in a few lines as hair then glue the pigtails into the holes.

Motorbike rocking horse

Roll a ball from 15 g of blue. Pinch the ends until they become longer and thinner, then bend as shown in the picture. Flatten two balls of 4 g of black slightly and use the ball tool to make an indentation on both sides. Glue a small ball of yellow into each and flatten slightly. Attach the wheels to the motorbike. Make two holes at the front and roll two footrests from black fondant with Tylose. Flatten a cone of 3 g of black for the saddle and secure it onto the motorbike.

Reinforce the pieces for the handlebars with Tylose and allow them to dry before assembling it. Roll 1 g of blue for the frame's tube. Roll a cylinder of yellow for the handlebars. Attach balls of black to both ends and roll a strip of black around both ends for the hand grips. Glue a yellow ball onto a black cone for the headlight. For the rear light, glue a ball of red onto a ball of black.

Coil strong yet flexible florist's wire around a stick to make a spring. Roll out a piece of grey fondant to a thickness of 1 cm and cut a square out of it for the concrete base. Insert the spring into it and secure the motorbike on top of it. Now assemble the handlebars and secure them, along with the lights and the footrests, onto the motorbike. If you wish, you can reinforce the handlebars with a short cocktail stick or a piece of spaghetti.

Pig rocking horse

Shape 15 g of pink into an oval. Make four holes underneath, one in each diagonal corner, for the legs and a hole on each side for the footrests. Coil strong yet flexible florist's wire around a stick to make a spring. Roll out a piece of grey fondant to a thickness of 1 cm and cut a square out of it

for the concrete base. Insert the spring into it and secure the pig's body on top of it. Roll out four pink cone shapes of 1 g each. Attach a black ball to each wide end for the trotters. Secure the legs in the holes in the pig's body, supporting the legs with pieces of sponge so that they stick properly. Roll two footrests from black fondant mixed with Tylose and secure them in the holes you made earlier.

Flatten a black sausage of 1 g for the saddle and attach this to the pig's back. Make a curly tail and allow it to dry. For the head, use a pink ball of 8 g and make holes in it for the ears. Flatten a ball of 1 g slightly for the nose. Make two holes for the nose and a mouth using the scallop tool, then attach the nose. Roll a tiny ball of white and slice it in half for the eyes. Glue them above the nose and add two black dots. Model two ears from two triangles and fix these into the holes. Secure the head onto the body, using a cocktail stick or spaghetti if you wish.

The finishing touches

Arrange the playground rides where you want them to be on the cake and trace around their bases with a needle tool. Remove these squares of fondant to reveal the drum. You can now insert the concrete bases in the gaps, so that they not only appear to be sitting in the grass, but they are also more stable too. Secure the schoolgirl in place using a cocktail stick and a bit of glue.

Make some pencils and books as extra decoration for the steps. For the books, roll out some white fondant and slice off a rectangular piece. Roll out a different colour of fondant thinner and slice off a piece that is slightly wider than the white piece. Slice one end straight and glue the white rectangle onto it. Fold it over the white piece and cut off any excess. Make an indentation in the folded side of the book to create a spine. For the pencils, roll out a strand of fondant in the colour of your choice. Attach a tiny dot of black onto a ball of yellow and model it into a cone shape, with the black dot as the point. Flatten the other end and attach it to the coloured strand.

Attach strands of green fondant in various places on the cake, not only around the base but also on and near the wall and by the steps. Now roughen the green fondant with a needle tool. You can cut small nicks or draw tiny circles in it, for example – you'll see that this creates a wonderfully 'distressed' texture so that the fondant takes on the appearance of greenery. Add a light dusting of green to create extra depth in the greenery if you wish. Finish by adding a few little flowers until you're completely happy with the final result.

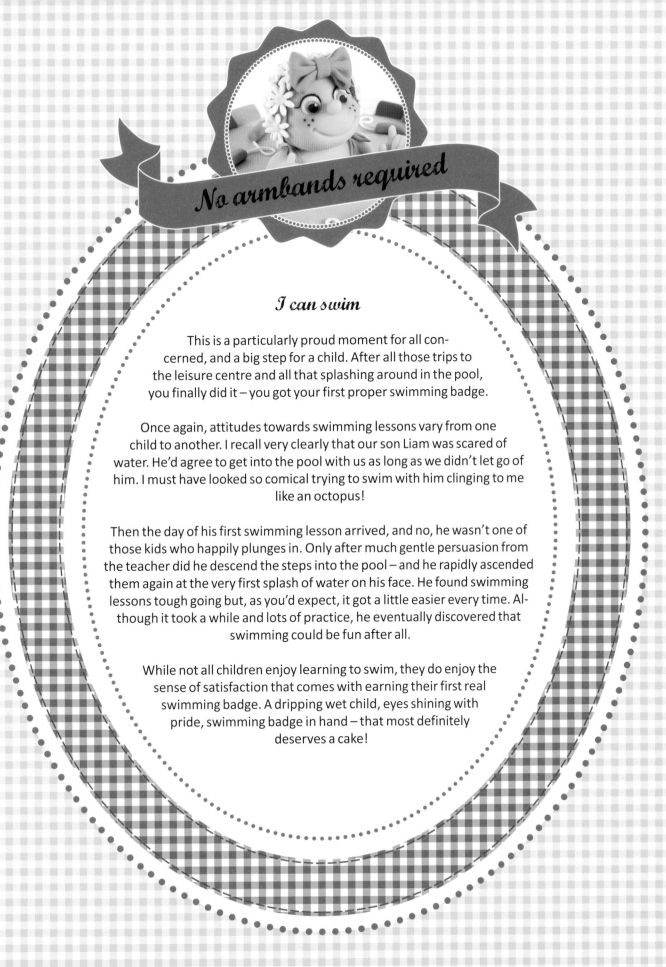

I can swim

This is a particularly proud moment for all concerned, and a big step for a child. After all those trips to the leisure centre and all that splashing around in the pool, you finally did it – you got your first proper swimming badge.

Once again, attitudes towards swimming lessons vary from one child to another. I recall very clearly that our son Liam was scared of water. He'd agree to get into the pool with us as long as we didn't let go of him. I must have looked so comical trying to swim with him clinging to me like an octopus!

Then the day of his first swimming lesson arrived, and no, he wasn't one of those kids who happily plunges in. Only after much gentle persuasion from the teacher did he descend the steps into the pool – and he rapidly ascended them again at the very first splash of water on his face. He found swimming lessons tough going but, as you'd expect, it got a little easier every time. Although it took a while and lots of practice, he eventually discovered that swimming could be fun after all.

While not all children enjoy learning to swim, they do enjoy the sense of satisfaction that comes with earning their first real swimming badge. A dripping wet child, eyes shining with pride, swimming badge in hand – that most definitely deserves a cake!

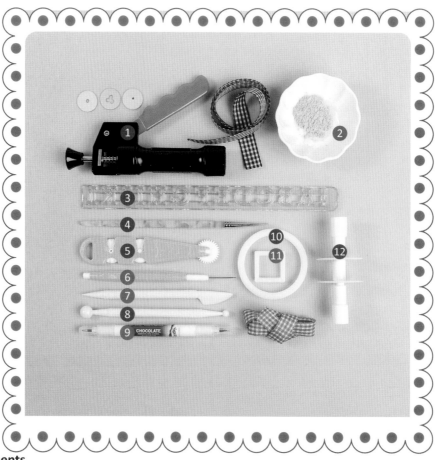

Requirements

Materials

* round cake drum of 25 cm
* a round filled and covered cake of 20 cm
* Tylose
2 pink dust
9 brown food decorating pen
* Tylose glue
* ribbon of your choice

Fondant

* 500 g light blue
* 200 g medium blue
* 100 g dark blue
* 100 g white
* little bit of black/red and some yellow if you're making the girl
* 120 g of flesh-coloured marzipan

Tools

1 sugarcraft gun with disc with middle-sized hole disc with smallest hole and small clover-shaped disc
3 alphabet & numbers tappits upper case (FMM)
4 brush
5 design wheeler 3 heads (stitching) (PME)
6 scriber needle tool (PME)
7 knife scriber tool (knife) (FMM)
8 ball tool (FMM)
10 round cutter 6 cm
11 square cutter 2.5 cm
12 multi ribbon cutter (FMM)

Tip: If you're struggling to squeeze the fondant through the smallest-holed disc on your sugarcraft gun, knead a little vegetable shortening such as Crisco through the fondant or heat it briefly in the microwave.

Tip: If your fondant tends to stick when rolling it up, place a sheet of baking paper on it before rolling.

Method

Place a circular piece of card which is 20 cm in diameter on the cake drum and trace around it carefully using a needle tool to leave a circle on the drum. Roll out the dark blue, medium blue, light blue and white fondant and cut out lots of squares from all of them using a 2.5 cm cutter. Attach them to the drum, alternating the colours to create a tiled floor. Make sure that you cover the entire surface of the drum outside of the circular line. Carefully trim the excess and attach a nice ribbon around the edge of the drum to finish it off. Cover any left-over squares with cling film to prevent them drying out.

Now take the filled and crumb-coated cake.

Roll out a strand of light blue fondant and place it around the uppermost edge of the cake to make the stand-up edge.

Roll out light blue fondant and cover the cake with it. Place the cake on the cake drum, surrounded by the tiled floor.

Taking the left-over squares, cut them so that they are tapered slightly and lay them along the top edge of light blue fondant, alternating the colours, with the narrow ends towards the centre.

Measure the circumference of your cake and roll out a strip of dark blue fondant to the correct length. Slice off a 1.5 cm strip using the ribbon cutter. Roll up the strip and use a little water to attach it to the side of the cake, just beneath the tiled edge.

Roll out a wider strip of medium blue to the same length. Cut the wave shapes using the template on page 130. Smooth out any unevenness and then attach the waves along the bottom edge of the cake. Roll out a thin strand of white or use the sugarcraft gun with the middle-sized disc to make strands. Use a fine paintbrush to apply some glue along the top edges of the waves then secure the white in place.

To make the rope for around the base of the cake, you can either roll out two strands and twist them together or you can use the small clover-shaped disc on the sugarcraft gun. This produces a ridged strand that you can twist to look like a rope. Attach the rope all the way round the cake.

Use the disc with the smallest hole to make the thin rope in the water, or you could roll out a very thin strand of white fondant instead. For the floats, roll out a strand of red to 7 mm in diameter and slice off 2 cm pieces. Soften the flat edges slightly and then glue them onto the white rope in the water.

Lifebelt

Knead a little Tylose through 40 g of white and roll it into a sausage of approximately 20 cm long. Slice off both ends straight then join them together to form a circle. Make some more of the rope as before. Arrange it loosely around the outside of the lifebelt and fix it in place at four points, starting at the join. Cut red strips of 1 cm in width and glue them onto the lifebelt at the four points where the rope is attached.

From dark blue fondant, cut out a circle 6 cm in diameter. Use a letter or number tappit or other cutter to decorate the centre of the blue circle as you wish. Then attach the lifebelt over the circle and allow it all to dry before securing it on the cake.

Boy

Roll a sausage from 30 g of flesh-coloured marzipan. Flatten this slightly against your work surface and gently pinch to create a short neck. Attach it to the cake using a skewer, making sure that part of the skewer protrudes so you can attach the head later. Model the boy's head from 70 g of flesh-coloured marzipan. Gently flatten half the face while rolling to create contours. Use the ball tool to create two eye sockets, which you can fill with two tiny balls of white, making sure you flatten them well into the face. Flatten two tiny balls of blue and attach them to the lower half of the eye-balls, then glue on black pupils. Finish off with a dot of white food colouring to add a twinkle. Use a knife to create a smiley mouth and make a hole for the nose. Roll a tiny cone for the nose and glue it in the hole. Draw three freckles on the cheeks using the brown food decorating pen. Dust the cheeks lightly with pink to create a healthy glow.

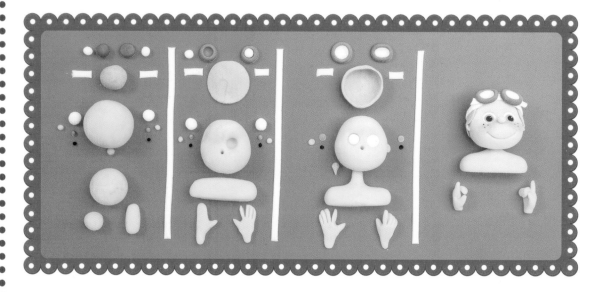

For the swimming cap, flatten a ball of 10 g of medium blue. Pinch along the edges and continue to stretch and pinch the swimming cap until it fits nicely over the head. Attach it and then use the design wheeler to add stitching.

For the goggles, use two balls of dark blue of 1 g each and make an indentation using your ball tool. Roll out two balls of white and insert them. Flatten with the ball tool and then pinch the balls into a slightly oval shape. Cut a strand of white and attach it around the edge of the swimming cap, then attach the goggles on top. Add two more pieces of white to the sides, then attach the head to the shoulders.

For each hand, take a small flesh-coloured roll of marzipan and flatten it slightly. Pinch to create a thumb just below the wrist. Extend the piece for the fingers and flatten it a bit more. Make three grooves for the fingers. Separate the forefingers from the rest and model them so that they're pointing, and bend the other three fingers into a fist. Angle the thumb towards the fingers. Flatten the wrists slightly and secure the hands on the cake.

But what if it's for a girl?!

I chose to make this cake for a boy, and the description above explains in detail how to make him. But with just a slight adjustment, he can be transformed into a girl – read on to see how easy it is.

Girl

To make a girl, simply follow the method for the boy but with the following changes:

Attach a thin strand of black fondant along the top edge of the eyes to make eyelashes. Replace the blue swimming cap with a red one, decorating it with white daisies with yellow centers and attaching a red bow to the front. For the swimsuit, use red fondant to make straps with bows on the shoulders.

Tip: If your young swimmer has a different skin tone, simply adapt the colour of the marzipan until you have the shade you need.

Time flies

Sweet 16

Before you know it, your little babies are all grown up. Needless to say, there are plenty of other milestones in a child's life that deserve to be honoured with a fabulous cake. But that would make this a really thick book, since there are just as many special occasions in an adult's life too. Which is why I've made this ten-year leap to my next special 'cake moment'.

I want to celebrate the key events in life with a cake and, let's face it, turning 16 is a momentous occasion for everyone. It's the birthday that signifies the end of your childhood and marks the start of the next stage of your journey, in a world of grown-ups.

I've really gone to town for this 16th birthday. A sizeable cake, which you could of course make on a smaller scale if you prefer – it still looks great with just two or three layers. When designing this cake, I thought back to the day that I turned 16 and yes, I celebrated it in true 80s' style. Back then, animal prints were everywhere and they're back in fashion today, so I thought it would be really fun to use zebra print in this cake design.

Sixteen is also the age of high-school crushes and, in my case, I still remember the lipstick-kisses on my mirror next to my sweetheart's photo. And while the world seems to have changed a lot since then, what with all the computers and smartphones, I'm sure that some aspects of being a teenage girl will forever remain the same.

Another thing I loved back then was masks, and I still do. I've amassed a considerable collection over the years, and while they were hard to come by when I was younger, nowadays you can even find them in garden centres every Christmas. I know that shoes and handbags are very popular themes for Sweet 16 cakes, but I fancied trying something a bit different – and after all, just like zebra print, masks are hip and trendy once again.

When you think of masks, you also think of feathers of course. I don't often use inedible items on my cakes but in this case the feathers were such a great addition to the design that I've made an exception. And for a Sweet 16 birthday, exceptions are most definitely allowed!

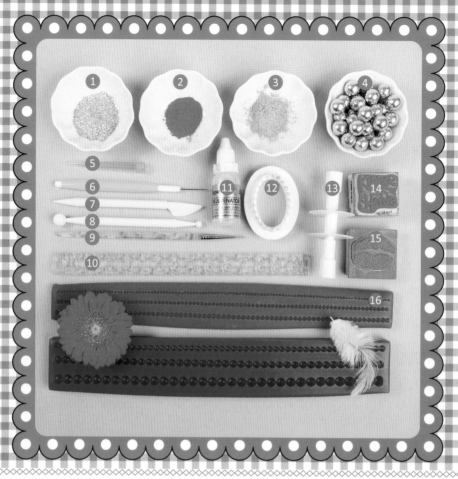

Requirements

Materials

* round cake drum of 40 cm
* 3 round filled and covered cakes of 35 cm/25 cm/15 cm
* 2 flower-shaped filled and covered cakes of 30 cm/20 cm
* grey and white royal icing in piping bags with small round nozzles
* feathers
① silver glitter (edible)
② red dust and silver dust ③
④ cola balls
⑤ 5 posy picks
⑪ rejuvenator spirit (alcohol)
* a polystyrene head or plain mask
* Tylose
* Tylose glue
* a ribbon of your choice

Fondant

* 1,400 g red
* 2,350 g white
* 400 g black

Tools

⑥ scriber needle tool (PME)
⑦ knife scriber tool (knife) (FMM)
⑧ ball tool (FMM)
⑨ brush
⑩ alphabet & numbers tappits upper case (FMM)
⑫ lips oval cutters
⑬ multi ribbon cutter (FMM)
⑭ stencil
⑮ letter stencil
⑯ perfect pearls moulds 10, 8, 6 mm (First Impressions) perfect pearls moulds 5, 4, 3 mm (First Impressions)

Method

Cover the drum with red fondant. Remove the central section of fondant from the drum as described in the explanation of the basics. Finish the drum off with a pretty ribbon.

I baked the round cakes higher than the flower-shaped ones to create a playful effect. The round cakes are 10 cm high after filling and covering while the flower-shaped ones are 7 cm high, but feel free to experiment.

Zebra print

For the zebra print, roll balls of fondant into sausages with a point at each end. Place them all in a plastic bag to prevent them drying out. Roll out white fondant until you have enough to cover the 35 cm cake. Place the black fondant sausages on top and carefully roll the whole thing flat (see photo as a guideline). To fill any big gaps, simply add extra sausages and roll out again. Cover the cake with the zebra print. Trim off the excess fondant and place the cake on the drum. Repeat this process for the small flower-shaped cake.

Cover both the round 15 cm cake and the large flower-shaped cake with red fondant. Cover the round 25 cm cake with white fondant. Now stack all the cakes as shown, making sure that both flower-shaped cakes have one of their curved petals pointing to the front.

Tip: Use the tables to work out the right quantities of fondant and refer to the basics when stacking and supporting the cake.

Tip: I really like the irregular zebra print, but if you prefer a neater pattern, first cover the cake with white, then roll out some black fondant and cut some stripes from it. You can then stick them onto the white cake as you please using a little water.

Cola balls

For a sparkly edge that tastes great too, I used cola balls (available from most sweet shops) – because I've never met a teenager who doesn't like cola, have you? Whenever you use cola balls, it's wise to warn people that they're very hard, so don't try to bite them!!! Use light grey royal icing to stick the cola balls around the bottom cake. Repeat this for the other zebra-print cake. If you prefer not to use cola balls, you can roll small balls of grey fondant through the silver dust instead. Using different-sized balls or balls covered in glitter can be a nice touch too. Or try alternating them with black, white and red balls to save you having to dust each and every silver ball.

String of pearls

For the next layer of cake, make strings of pearls in black, white and red using the 8 mm pearl mould. First attach the red pearls around the lowest red cake. Secure the black and then the white pearls directly above them.

Tip: Practice using the rubber stamps a few times on a spare piece of fondant.

Rubber stamps

Rubber stamps are a quick and easy way to add extra effect to your cake, such as here with the lipstick kisses and text. You can use any stamps you like to decorate your cake – there are hundreds of different ones available online, and you can even design your own. In this case, mix some red colour powder with rejuvenator spirit to create a red dye and allow a piece of sponge to absorb the dye. Dab the dye onto your lipstick kiss stamp, taking care that you don't use too much, and then gently press it against the cake for a few seconds. Do the same for the text.

Measure the circumference of the cake with the lipstick kisses on it and roll out a strip of black to the same length. Sprinkle some glitter on it and roll it again to secure the glitter in place. Cut two ribbons from it using the ribbon cutter and attach one of them around the base of the cake.

Pendant

Starting at the front, attach the second black ribbon around the base of the top round cake, allowing both ends to come to a point in the centre of the flower-shaped cake's protruding petal below. You can now hang a pendant from the ribbon. To make the pendant, cut out differently sized ovals using the cutters and stick them one on top of the other. Use the tappits to cut out the number 16 and stick it on top. Brush the number with a little glue and use a damp paintbrush to apply some glitter to it. Finish the pendant off with a bow.

Tip: There are countless moulds available for pendants and medals, so feel free to use one of those instead.

Glitter chain and pearl necklace

Make the glitter chain by pressing a thin strand of grey fondant into the 4 mm pearl mould. Attach the chain around the red top cake. Cut out the word 'SWEET' using the tappits and stick each letter directly below the chain with a tiny bead in between. Brush the letters and the chain with a little glue and then use a damp paintbrush to apply some glitter to them. Hold a sheet of kitchen paper beneath the brush to prevent the whole cake becoming covered in glitter.

For the pearl necklace above the glitter chain, use the 6 mm pearl mould. Make a loop too, sticking a few extra pearls over the join, to create the effect of a knot.

Roses, bow and feathers

Make a bow as described in the method for the engagement cake, but this time using zebra-print fondant as outlined above. Allow the bow to dry thoroughly before using royal icing to secure it to the 'lipstick kisses' cake.
For the roses, roll out a piece of red fondant and fold it in half lengthways, not too tightly, into a strip. Now loosely roll up the strip, making an indentation now and again to give the roses their shape. Pinch together at the base and trim off the excess fondant. Make nine in total, in varying sizes.

Make four small plumes of black and white feathers. Put a little fondant into the posy pick and insert the feathers into it. Place the posy picks into the cakes as shown in the photo. Attach one rose to the top plume of feathers and two roses to the feathers below. Attach three to the feathers on the zebra-print cake and four roses to the feathers on the cake drum. Ensure that the holes the posy picks have made in the cakes are no longer visible.

Mask

Knead some Tylose through white fondant. Cut the mask from the fondant using the template on page 133 as a guideline, but feel free to adapt the design. Add points, draw the shape of a butterfly – let your imagination run riot!

To help the mask retain the right shape while drying, you can buy a plain mask from a craft shop or use a polystyrene head as I've done here – they're not expensive and can be reused. If you're feeling particularly creative, you can even use it to make a full-face mask – for if you're planning a Halloween cake, for example, or perhaps a Phantom mask to celebrate a theatre performance.

Allow the mask to dry thoroughly and leave it on the polystyrene head while decorating it to prevent it breaking. Paint the forehead silver using silver dust mixed with rejuvenator spirit.

Roll out thin strands of black and attach them to the sides of the mask in a zebra print. Pipe some royal icing in a zigzag pattern around the eyeholes. Sprinkle with glitter.

Decorate the silver forehead section by piping some swirls of royal icing. Decorate the white part below the eyes with swirls and dots of royal icing as you wish, and paint on some silver dots. As a finishing touch, pipe some royal icing in a zigzag pattern around the mask's edges.

Make two small roses by rolling one half of the length of a strip of red slightly flatter. By then rolling the strip up in a straight line, the thinner half will remain slightly open to form a flower. Pinch together at the base and trim off the excess with scissors. Attach the roses to the mask using a dot of royal icing.

Place the mask upright onto the cake and attach two strips of black fondant as ribbons. Arrange them playfully for extra realism.

Insert a posy pick containing feathers into the cake behind the mask to create the illusion that the feathers are attached to it.

Tip: In view of the time needed for the fondant and the royal icing to dry, it's best to make the mask beforehand.

School's out

Graduation day

Congratulations, you've passed!
Passing your exams is another of the most
important steps in life.

Whether marking the end of high school or graduation
from university, passing your exams and receiving that
much-coveted diploma is worth a cupcake at the very least.
Needless to say, you can make this design into a full-scale cake
too, but what's wrong with cupcakes? After all, not only are
they easier to hand out if you want to celebrate your achieve-
ments together with your fellow students, but they're also fun to
make and a lot less work, which will be a welcome relief after all
those weeks of revising.

While I've kept the cupcakes really small and made mini-cupcakes, you can make them bigger if you prefer. The method is
the same, but the mini-cupcakes mean you can fit more of
them in the oven at once.

Whatever size you decide to make, don't forget to
choose a really tasty recipe (or cake mix) when baking them. Because as well as looking fantastic,
cupcakes – just like large cakes – should be
simply delicious.

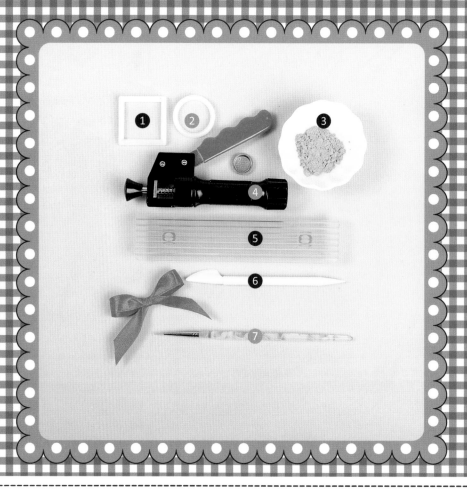

Materials
* mini-cupcakes or regular cupcakes
* apricot jam
3 gold dust
* silver cupcake cases

Fondant
* red
* yellow
* white
* black

Tools
1 square cutter
2 round cutter
4 sugarcraft gun with small-holed disc
5 strip cutter no. 2 (Jem)
6 knife scriber tool (knife) (FMM)
7 brush

Cupcake basics

A good cupcake starts with the basis – how it's baked. To bake your cupcakes, use a tasty recipe; I don't list any recipes here, because there are hundreds of great recipe books out there, as well as loads of fantastic recipes to be found on the internet and in peoples' blogs.

Plus I have to admit that I often choose the easy option when it comes to making cupcakes. I usually use a ready-made cupcake mix, and there are plenty of delicious variations available. It's quick and easy and, believe me, I've never had anyone complain as they sink their teeth into one of my gooey brownie cupcakes or yummy caramel cupcakes. Or how about cupcakes made with a strawberry mix, or chocolate, or orange...need I go on?!

The key to nice, even cupcakes is to bake them in a cupcake baking tin. Tins are available for both regular-sized and mini-cupcakes.

For this design, and actually for any cupcake occasion, it's best if all the cupcakes are of equal height and have a nice flat upper surface, which is why I fill the cupcake cases using a disposable piping bag.

To ensure the upper surface turns out flat, set aside a glass chopping board while the cupcakes are baking. Once the cupcakes are ready, take them out of the oven and immediately place the glass chopping board on top of them. Turn the whole thing over and gently remove the baking tin from the cupcakes. Leave the cupcakes upside down to cool for a while. This gives them a nice smooth top surface and the cases stay in place too. When the next batch of cupcakes is almost ready to come out of the oven, turn the slightly cooled cupcakes the right way up and place them onto a rack to finish cooling.

If you want to decorate the cupcakes with fondant or marzipan, you'll need something to stick it with. You can use buttercream, royal icing or piping gel, but I prefer to use apricot gel, which I make by pureeing apricot jam with a blender. This turns it into a finely structured apricot gel which is easy to brush on. It not only forms a nice, transparent base for the decorations, but it tastes delicious too.

And now we're ready to start decorating...

Diploma cupcake

If you're celebrating passing your high-school exams, or perhaps making cupcakes for someone else, it's nice to decorate them with mini-diplomas. They're quick and easy to make, which is an extra bonus if you're making lots to share with your friends.

Bake the cupcakes in the size of your choice – regular or mini – in silver cases. That looks particularly chic in contrast with the black fondant, but you can of course use a different colour if you prefer.

Take a cutter that is slightly larger than the diameter of your cupcakes. Roll out black fondant or marzipan and cut circles from it. Stick the circles onto the cupcakes using a little apricot gel, pressing the edges down neatly.

Roll out white fondant and cut out a square. How big? That depends on the size of your cupcakes. Experiment to find out which size of cutter works best, or you can of course cut out the squares by hand instead. Roll up the squares loosely and curl the edges up for extra effect.

Roll out red fondant and cut off strips, either by hand or using the strip cutter.

Wrap a red strip around each diploma and stick a bow onto it.

Mortar boards

One thing that literally screams 'I passed' is of course a mortar board. We've all seen images of students tossing them into the air en-masse after their graduation ceremony, and this typically British and American tradition is becoming increasingly popular in other parts of the world too.

To make the mortar boards, remove the cases from the cupcakes. Turn the cupcakes upside down and brush them all over with apricot gel. Roll out black fondant and cover the cupcakes with it. Use a round cutter to remove the excess fondant in one go to ensure a neat edge. For the top part, roll out the black fondant and cut out a square. How big? Once again, it depends on the size of your cupcakes. Experiment to find out which size of cutter works best, or you can of course cut out the squares by hand instead. As soon as they are dry, stick the squares onto the cupcake.

Knead some Crisco through a piece of yellow fondant and fill the sugarcraft gun with it. Fit the disc with lots of tiny holes and squeeze the fondant through it. Slice it into small clumps which you pinch together at one end to form tassels. Stick a small ball of yellow onto the tassel and make a hole in it. For the top part, roll a thin sausage of yellow, rolling it into a point at one end which you attach into the hole. Dust lightly with gold and attach it onto the mortar board, allowing the tassel to dangle over the side. Finish off by sticking a small ball of black in the centre of the mortar board.

Tip: Make the squares for on top beforehand and allow them to dry thoroughly on both sides.

A place of your own

Maybe you got your first place before you graduated? Perhaps you got married first and then moved into your own house? Maybe you didn't bother with the wedding, and just set up home with your partner? Or you might even still live at home with your parents.

Whatever path your life follows, there comes a time when you have to stand on your own two feet. Ultimately, everyone dreams of a place of their own.

Whether your first home is a student flat or a mid-terraced house, three floors up or an idyllic country cottage with white picket fence, or maybe even a penthouse apartment – none of that really matters. Your first home is always special, simply because it's yours. Which is a great reason for a party, and every party warrants a delicious cake.

For this cake, I've chosen an entirely white design in the shape of a music box, because of the symbolism of receiving 'the key of the door' and the purity of entering a new phase of your life. The design was also inspired by the thought of white picket fences and a sense of belonging. I've incorporated all of these elements yet created a relatively simple and modest cake. After all, understated colours and designs can sometimes be just as effective, don't you agree?

Even if it's years since you first got your own place, this is of course a wonderful cake to make for someone else. It's also the ideal 'moving in' gift to celebrate someone's new home.

Requirements
Materials

* round cake drums of 10 cm 12.5 cm and 22.5 cm
* 2 round filled and covered cakes, 20 cm and 15 cm
1 silverdust
3 rejuvenator spirit (alcohol)
4 sparkle dust
12 silver florist's wire
* royal icing
* Tylose
* Tylose glue
* ribbon of your choice

Fondant

* 1,000 g of white
* grey

Tools

2 dust brush
5 gate cutter (Jem)
6 possibly a bush mould (FPC)
7 ball tool (FMM)
8 knife scriber tool (knife) (FMM)
9 piping nozzle tip 12 (Wilton)
10 scriber needle tool (PME)
11 brush
13 straight frill cutter no. 3

Method

Place the 20 cm cake on the cake drum and cover both the cake and the drum in one go. Attach a pretty ribbon around the drum and attach the same ribbon to the 10 cm cake drum.

Cover both the 15 cm cake and the 12.5 cm cake drum with white fondant. Stack the cakes as shown and fix the 10 cm cake drum in place on top of the top cake. You can place a few dowels underneath if you wish, but not too many, because what's going on top is relatively light.

House

Cut out all the elements of the house using the templates. Cut out small windows, either by hand or using a small square cutter. In the house's two front-facing walls, cut out a small circle in the point of the gable. Place some firm royal icing in a piping bag using the nozzle with a small hole. Place the house elements face down. Pipe a small cross at each window and allow the icing and the house elements to dry thoroughly. Cut out the two roof elements and use the straight frill cutter no. 3 (wavy edge) to make a roof-tile pattern in them.

Now stick the sides, front and back of the house together using royal icing and allow it to dry for a while. Then stick the two roof sections onto the house and allow to dry. Stick the sides of the porch to the front of the porch and then stick the whole thing up against the house's front wall. Allow it to dry before you attach the smooth roof sections onto the porch. Stick the chimney elements together and then attach it all in place on the main roof.

Bushes

You can use a mould to make the bushes but, as you can see in the photo, they're not difficult to make by hand if you don't happen to have a suitable mould.

For the pointy bush, roll 3 g into a carrot shape and flatten it. Cut three notches in the outer edge at an angle. Create texture on the surface of the bush by pricking holes in it with a needle tool (or using a small wire brush).

For the flowerpot, roll a cone of 2.5 g. Flatten it slightly and slice it into three pieces, using the middle piece as the lower part of the flowerpot.

For the upper edge, cut out a circle of 3 cm, slice off a small part and turn this so its curved edge is pointing upwards, then stick it onto the flowerpot. You can make three edges from each circle. For the round bush, cut out a circle of 3 cm. Smooth the edges and give the bush some texture by pricking holes in it with a needle tool. Make the stem by sticking a thin strand between the flowerpot and the circular bush.

Cat

For the cat's body, flatten a cone of 1 g. Make an incision to form the front paw and cut a notch in the rounded part to make the back leg, then draw the shape of the haunch in the fondant above it. Flatten a ball of 0.5 g to make the cat's head. Pinch into the shape of two ears and make two holes for the eyes. Attach a tiny nose and then stick the head to the body. Roll out a tail and fix it in place.

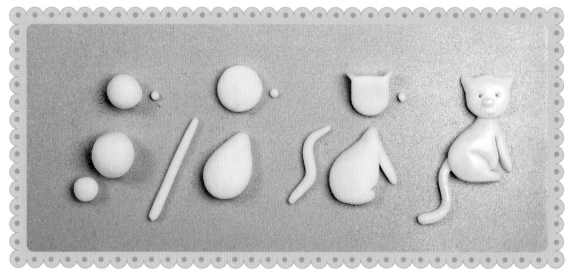

White picket fence

For the picket fence, knead some Tylose through a piece of white fondant and then roll it out thinly. Allow the fondant to dry a little on both sides before cutting out the fence using the Jem gate cutter. You may need to remove the fence from the cutter in parts, using the needle tool, but don't worry if so, because it's easier to attach it to the cake in several sections. I haven't used the cutter's gate pattern on this cake, but you can if you wish.

On cloud nine and key of the door

Cut off three pieces of florist's wire to the required length and bend the ends into a slight hook shape to prevent the cloud sliding down over the point. To make the clouds, flatten an oval of approximately 1.5 g and make five notches around the edge with your knife. Flatten the cloud again and then attach it over a hook of silver wire. Press some fondant into the chimney and insert the pieces of wire with the clouds on them into it.

Cut out a square of 2.5 cm. Use piping nozzle no. 12 to make a hole in it for the keyhole and cut downwards slightly from the bottom of the hole. Stick tiny balls at the corners and score a tiny line on each of them so they look like screws. Stick the keyhole onto the cake.

Cut out a circle of grey using the back of piping nozzle no. 12 and make a hole in it using the other end of the nozzle, but don't make it too thin. Stick a tiny ball of grey into it. Roll a tiny ball of fondant around a damp cocktail stick. Stick another ball of fondant onto it and then attach the key head. Dust the key with silver and allow it to dry. Wait until the last possible moment to place it in the lock.

Full colour?

If you're not keen on the all-white design, you can make this cake using pre-coloured fondant or paint it using a range of shimmer powders instead. Feel free to adapt it in line with your own ideas – after all, it's your cake!

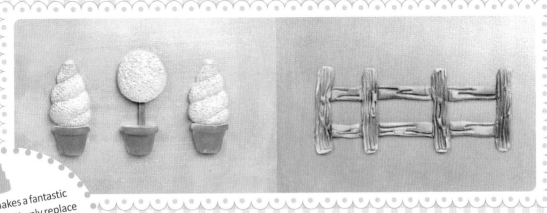

Tip: This cake makes a fantastic Christmas cake too. Simply replace the bushes with Christmas trees and use royal icing to decorate the house, bushes and fence with snow. Make some fondant snowballs and stick them around the edge of the cake. And while it looks gorgeous in colour, it's particularly festive in white.

Engagement cake

For many people, of course, getting married is one
of the most significant steps they take in life. And we'll
cover that step soon...but first things first!

Because before they get married, most couples get engaged,
and that's often coupled with an engagement party. And there
it is once again: a great reason to celebrate with a cake and
hence for us a perfect excuse to make one.

Thinking of skipping the engagement phase?

Then there's always the moment that you tell your parents (and
prospective in-laws) about your marriage plans. And what
could be a nicer way of breaking the news than to place this
cake on the coffee table when you've invited them round
for a seemingly innocent cup of coffee. As they turn to
look at you, their faces filled with surprise and astonishment, it's the ideal time to share the joy and
shout out:

Mum, Dad...we're getting married!!!

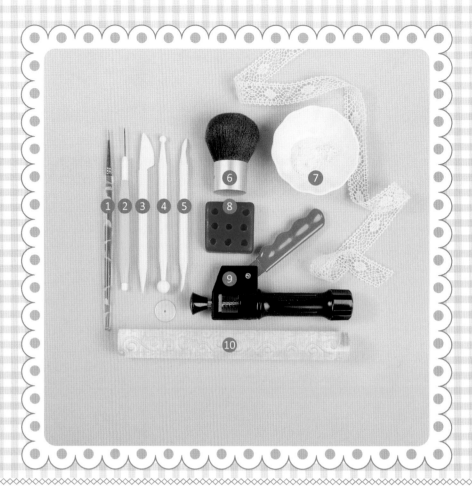

Materials

* round cake drum of 30 cm
* 1 cake baked in the wonder mould
* 1 piece of cake cardboard
* dowels
* long wooden cake dowel
* Tylose glue
* ribbon of your choice
7 sparkledust

Fondant

* 1,000 g white
* 300 g black

Tools

1 brush
2 scriber needle tool (PME)
3 knife scriber tool (knife) (FMM)
4 balltool
5 flute vein tool (FMM)
6 dust brush
* closed scallop serrated crimper 3/4 (PME)
* moulds for perfect pearls 5, 4, 3 mm (First Impressions),
8 Moulds Itty Bitty Roses/9 (First Impressions)
9 sugarcraft gun using disk with small holes
10 impression roller or impression mat

Method

Cover the cake drum with the black fondant, attach a pretty ribbon around it and set it aside to dry.

Bake the sponge in a wonder mould as required. Slice the sponge in half horizontally. Take a cardboard in the required size. Cut a 2 cm hole in the centre and place the top half of the sponge on top of it. Roll out a piece of marzipan and cut out a circle that fits onto the lower half of the cake. Cover the top of the lower half with buttercream and stick the piece of fondant onto it. Then use a cake saw to slice both halves of the cake two or three times horizontally. Fill them as you wish, but not too thickly – it's better to fill them three times with a thin layer of filling than twice with a thick one. Place the top of the skirt on the lower part of the cake and crumb-coat the cake with buttercream.

When you come to cut the cake, you can now slice smaller pieces rather than needing a dinner plate to accommodate such a huge slice of cake, plus the filling is more evenly distributed per portion. Also, the cake has more layers which means that the skirt stands taller and yet still retains its shape nicely.

Tip: If your sponge is very soft, insert four dowels into the lower cake before placing the upper part on top of it.

The skirt

Use a tape measure to measure the height of your cake, since this can of course vary each time. For the underskirt, roll out approximately 200 g of fondant. Cut out a triangle to the height as just measured. The lower edge should be approximately 20 cm wide and slightly curved, as in the photo. Make a pattern of your choice on the top part of the triangle using an impression roller or impression mat. Leave the bottom 5 cm smooth. Pinch the bottom edge of the fondant with the crimper to make a decorative edge along the bottom. Repeat this 5 cm higher along the bottom edge of the pattern. Now you can use the crimper on the smooth section between the two crimped edges. Alternate the angle of the crimper in the fondant to create a lace effect. Then stick the underskirt onto the front of the cake.

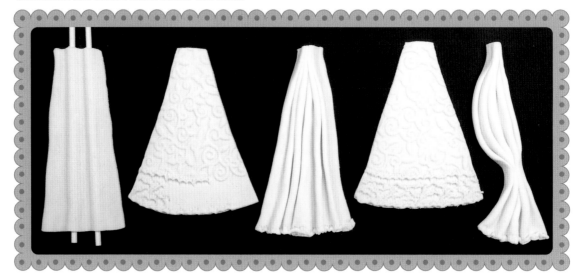

Pleats

For the pleated skirt, roll out several pieces of fondant to approximately 12 cm in width, making the pieces about two centimetres longer than the underskirt. If you want sharp pleats, allow the fondant pieces to flare slightly towards the hem. Place two or three skewers lengthways beneath the fondant and press the fondant gently downwards between the skewers. Push the skewers closer together at the top and then remove them from under the fondant. Then pinch the fondant together at the top and crimp the lower edge. Attach the fondant to the back of the skirt, in the centre. To ensure that you'll finish nice and neatly at the front, begin precisely at the rear centre – otherwise you might end up slightly off-centre.

Repeat the steps above but with one difference: this time, first fold the side edge that will adjoin the previous piece of skirt inwards before you start making the pleats. This way, when you attach the new piece onto the previous piece, the fold will serve as an extra pleat, making an almost invisible join between the skirt sections. Cover the entire skirt in this way until the front just reaches the underskirt.

Tip: Make sure that all the
leats are neatly finished at the
p edge – the bodice will disguise
some unevenness but it won't
cover much. But the bow at the
back can of course be useful
to hide any minor flaws.

Now make two more pieces but this time folding both side edges inwards. Decide the height at which you want the skirt to be swept open and held back at the front. Pinch the fondant gently at this height and then attach the final two pleated sections onto the cake. To decorate those points, make roses, either by hand or using the itty bitty rose mould, or attach a bow as you prefer.

The bodice and shoulders

Roll out a ball of 80 g of white fondant into roughly a cone shape. Hold the cone in your hand with the wider end pointing upwards, allowing the top third to protrude. Now place your finger on top at an angle and press forwards and downwards. This will push the top part over your hand slightly to form the bosom. Carefully smooth out any unevenness. Pinch around the indentation to create a slightly raised edge. Flatten the bottom of the bodice and pull the bottom edge outwards slightly all the way round. Create a narrower waist by rolling with your finger just below the bosom.

Roll a sausage from approximately 30 g of black fondant. Pinch it carefully to create a neck and flatten the neck at the top. Flatten both ends too or slice a piece off if the sides extend too far. Attach the shoulders and neck to the white bodice, smoothing out any joins. Flatten two tiny balls and attach these to the sides. Make holes in them to look like stitches on a dressmaker's dummy. Add to the effect by making stitches along the top of the shoulders seams and down the middle of the neck at the front and back too. It's these details that make all the difference to your cake. Roll a ball of black thinner in the middle and flatten one end so that it looks like a pawn, then attach this onto the neck.

Use a long wooden dowel to make a hole from the base of the torso up through the centre until two-thirds of the way up. Remove the dowel and then insert it down through the centre of the skirt until it touches the cake drum underneath the cake. Now place the torso onto it and glue it in place.

Roll out a piece of white fondant for the front part of the dress and make the same pattern on it as you made on the underskirt. Cut out a rectangular shape that is slightly wider at the top and is the same length as the bodice's height.

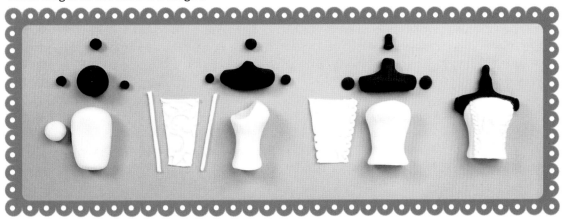

Roll out two strands and attach them down the sides of this panel. Make a tiny incision every couple of millimetres and then use a flute vein tool to create a decoratively textured edge. Then attach the panel to the front of the bodice and finish off the lower edge with a strand of white fondant.

Make tiny roses by hand or using the itty bitty rose mould and decorate the top edge of the bodice with them.

Finishing touches

As the finishing touches for the cake, you can roll tiny balls to make a string of pearls around the mannequin's neck, either by hand or using the 3 mm pearl mould.

If you prefer to model a closed fastening, you can use the same kind of pearls at the back of the bodice, but I personally like the lace-up effect. To make it, roll out thin strands of fondant and attach them in a criss-cross pattern, ending with a bow. You can of course also use a sugarcraft gun for this.

As a final detail at the rear of the dress, attach a gorgeous bow. First cut out two sashes, slicing a wedge out of the end of each one before you attach them playfully to the dress. For the bow itself, roll out a rectangle of 10 cm x 6 cm. Fold both edges inwards lengthways. Brush some glue in the centre and fold both ends to meet in the middle. Turn it over and make two pleats in the centre. Take a strip of 6 cm x 1.5 cm and fold both edges inwards lengthways, press together slightly and glue this strip over the centre of the other piece to form the bow. Then attach the bow to the cake just below the bodice and sit back and enjoy all the compliments you'll undoubtedly receive for this amazing cake.

Tip: Make the dress in pink or purple, or use a mix of different colours. I bet you know a little girl who'd be over the moon to receive a birthday cake like this.

The big day

Wedding cake

And then finally, the big day has arrived – your wedding day. Funnily enough, I've never been married. While we've been together for more than 25 years, we never seem to have got round to getting married. Not that I really mind – I feel just as married as the next woman by now. But it does mean that I've never had the chance to make a splendid wedding cake for myself. Although who knows, that day might still come! Luckily, I've had plenty of opportunities to make fabulous cakes for my family and friends, as well as for countless couples who've ordered their wedding cakes from me in the past.

While making a cake for such an important day is always a bit nerve-racking, it's all worthwhile when you see the look of sheer bliss on the newlyweds' faces as they're standing there, cutting the cake and revelling in feeding pieces of it to each other.

In the past few years, I've noticed that more and more people are reversing the trend. Instead of getting first engaged, then married and only then thinking about having children, a growing number of couples are already parents by the time they say "I do". And as a result, many of the weddings I've attended recently have been 'child-friendly' occasions.

I've also noticed that many people are opting for an 'adult' filling in their cake, such as fruit-based fillings containing a dash of liqueur for extra flavour. Chocolate cakes are becoming more popular too, with a rum and cherry filling, for instance, or one of my personal favourites: a Baileys filling. But that means that the children can't eat the cake. You could of course make some yummy cupcakes for the kids, but I realised last time that most children prefer to get a slice of that big, impressive-looking cake. And if lots of children are going to be present, why not make an extra cake especially for them? One that complements the adult cake, but perhaps with a child-friendly twist.

Another thing we're seeing more of at weddings is a big cake for the bride and groom to slice and miniature versions for each individual guest. A wonderfully luxurious idea, but also one that involves an immense amount of work, especially if you need 200 of them.

This wedding cake includes all of my ideas in one design: a five-layer wedding cake for the bride and groom, a matching children's cake with a cute take on the bride and groom, and mini-cakes for all the guests.

In terms of the design, I've not gone for a particularly traditional look. A wedding cake doesn't have to be the classic white with piped royal icing, of course. These soft pastel shades exude romance too, and nowadays literally anything goes. A smaller version of this wedding cake would also make a lovely treat for Mother's Day or a birthday.

Requirements
Materials
* round cake drum of 37.5 cm
* 5 round filled and covered cakes of 30 cm/25 cm/ 20 cm/15 cm/10 cm
❹ pink, green and mother-of-pearl candy beads 7 mm (SK)
* royal icing
* Tylose
* Tylose glue
* ribbon of your choice

Fondant
* 450 g white
* 1,000 g grey
* 350 g green
* 650 g pink

Children's wedding cake
Materials
* cake drum of 25 cm
* 2 round filled and covered cakes of 20 cm/15 cm

Fondant
* 350 g green
* 450 g pink
* 250 g grey
* little bit of white

Tools
❶ daisy plunger large (PME)
❷ flower blossom plunger sizes M and XL (PME)
❸ sugarcraft gun (disc with middle-sized hole)
❺ scriber needle tool (PME)
❻ flute vein tool (FMM)
❼ ball tool (FMM)
❽ knife scriber tool (knife) (FMM)
❾ brush
❿ flower foam pad (PME)

Extra tools
closed scallop serrated crimper 3/4 (PME)

Method for main wedding cake

Cover the drum with white fondant. Remove the centre of the fondant from the drum as described in the basics. Finish off the drum with a nice, matching ribbon.

Cover the largest and the smallest cakes with grey fondant. Cover the 25 cm cake with pink, the 20 cm cake with white and the 15 cm cake with green, although you can change the colour sequence if you prefer. Then stack all cakes as required, as described in the basics.

Around the base of each cake, I've applied candy beads, which are large beads that taste like a candy necklace. They're not too hard and are available in loads of different colours, both matt and shiny. I've stuck them on one by one using a little bit of royal icing. If you don't want to be bothered with this or don't have time, you can of course make a string of pearls using a pearl mould.

For the second and third layers, roll out all four pieces of the coloured fondant and allow them to dry slightly on both sides. Use the largest blossom plunger to cut flowers from all of them. Place the flowers on a flower foam pad and press the ball tool into each petal to curl them a little. Make an indentation in the centre too and then attach a ball of fondant in a contrasting colour of your choice. Although I've not done it here, you can use the candy beads for this instead if you prefer. On the pink cake, I've attached the flowers in groups of three and on the green cake I've attached them individually to form a regular pattern. If you prefer a neater cake, use that pattern on the pink cake too.

To make the swirls on the top, middle and bottom cake, use the sugarcraft gun and the disc with the middle-sized hole. Knead some Crisco through the fondant to make it easier to squeeze.

Tip: You can make all the flowers in advance but once they've dried they won't stick using Tylose glue. Attach them using dots of royal icing instead.

Draw the swirls on the cake using a scriber needle tool – in other words, score the lines in faintly. Then paint over the lines with Tylose glue and carefully apply the thin strands of fondant on top. It's worth taking your time to do this neatly.

For the leaves, roll out the green fondant and cut out daisies using the large daisy plunger. Separate the leaves into ones or twos. Make tiny incisions in them and pinch them together slightly at the base. Then stick these leaves randomly onto the swirls. Use the medium blossom plunger to cut out tiny flowers and use the middle part of the plunger to immediately stick them onto the leaves to make clusters of one, two or three flowers.

As you can see, a wedding cake doesn't have to be difficult to be beautiful. It's always a good idea to use a design that looks effective but is not too complicated to make, especially if you're making your own cake. Making the flowers in advance can also save you a lot of precious time. I'm sure you've got enough on your plate organising your wedding, so it's nice if decorating your cake can be a stress-free rather than stressful process.

Method for children's wedding cake

Cover the cake drum with grey fondant and finish it off with the same ribbon you used around the adult cake. You can also add a bow if you wish.

Cover the 20 cm cake with pink fondant and the 15 cm cake with green. Stack the cakes on the drum as required and attach the candy beads around their bases.

Use the same disc as before to make the green stems for the bottom cake. Make the leaves in the same way and stick them onto the stems. Make the flowers for the tops of the stems in the same way as above too. The only difference is that here I've kept all the flowers white and attached green, pink or grey centres instead.

Cow bride

Make the bride's dress by rolling a cone of 70 g of white and flattening the wider end. Use the crimper to add a decorative edge. A quarter of the way down the body, draw a line all the way around and make some grooves below it to create the effect of pleats in the dress.

For each sleeve, roll a cone of 3.5 g. Draw three lines at an angle at the wider end of the sleeve. Stick a tiny ball of white on top and flatten it, creating the effect of gathered cuffs. Cut 1.5 g of black in half and make two tiny balls for the hooves. Flatten them slightly and make a notch on one side of each, then stick them to the cuffs. Cut two notches halfway along the arms and bend them into shape, one slightly more than the other. Attach the arms to the dress. To make the collar, flatten a ball of 1 g of white and cut a notch in it, then attach it to the front of the dress.

To make the head, roll a ball from 18 g of white. Roll two black pointy cones of 1 g each. Flatten them and stick them over both sides of the head with the points towards each other. Insert a cocktail stick into the body and then attach and glue the head to the body.

For the face, roll a white sausage of 1 g and flatten it slightly. Roll a sausage from 1 g of pink and make a dent on one side before flattening it. Stick the pink part onto the white part and then attach it to the cow's head. Draw a line for the mouth towards the bottom of the face and open the bottom lip slightly using a flute vein tool. Use this to make nostrils at an angle too. Roll two tiny balls of white for the eyes. Flatten them and then add a slightly smaller ball of black that's been flattened. Roll tiny balls of white for a twinkle in the eye, or add a dot of white food colouring instead.

For the ears, use one black and one white cone and flatten them. Press a smaller pink cone onto each of them. Use a flute vein tool to make a dent and pinch the lower edges together to form ears. Make two holes in the head and insert the ears into them.

Tip: Don't be afraid to make quite large holes for the ears. This will allow you to insert them further into the head, so they'll stay in place better.

Make really tiny pink roses by rolling out a strip of fondant and flattening it along one edge lengthways. Then roll up the strip neatly. The thinner edge will remain slightly open. Pinch the lower edge together and use scissors to trim off any excess.

For the bride's veil, roll out a piece of 5 cm x 8 cm. Crimp a decorative edge on one side and gather the other edge into pleats, then attach the pleated edge onto the head. Make leaves as described above and fix them, together with the roses, onto the veil.

Stick a tiny ball of green into the bride's hoof and then cover it with leaves and roses to create a miniature bridal bouquet.

Cow groom

Make a cone from 35 g of black. Make a cut from the wider edge to halfway in. Rub the sharp edges to smooth them and make the rounded shape of trouser legs. Then flatten the bottom edge. Score a line just above the lower edge of each trouser leg to create the effect of turn-ups. To make the black hooves, slightly flatten two balls of 1.5 g. Make a notch in each of the hooves and attach them under the trouser legs. Make a cone of 7 g of grey for the jacket. Working from the wider edge, hollow it out a little and then attach the jacket to the trousers. Draw a line down the front as the fastener. For the collar, flatten a ball of 1 g of grey and cut out a notch, then stick it onto the jacket.

To make each sleeve, roll a cone from 3.5 g of white. Attach a tiny ball of white to the wider end and flatten it. Cut 1.5 g in half and use it to make two tiny balls for the hooves. Flatten the balls slightly and cut notches on one side, then attach the hooves to the cuffs. Cut two notches halfway along both arms and bend them into shape, one slightly more than the other. Attach the arms to the body.

To make the head, roll a ball from 18 g of white. Roll two black pointy cones of 1 g each. Flatten them and stick them over both sides of the head with the points towards each other. Insert a cocktail stick into the body and then attach and glue the head to the body.

For the face, roll a white sausage of 1 g and flatten it slightly. Roll a sausage from 1 g of pink and make a dent on one side before flattening it. Stick the pink part onto the white part and then attach it to the cow's head. Draw a line for the mouth towards the bottom of the face and open the bottom lip slightly using a flute vein tool. Use this to make nostrils at an angle too. Roll two tiny balls of white for the eyes. Flatten them and then add a slightly smaller ball of black that's been flattened. Roll tiny balls of white for a twinkle in the eye, or add a dot of white food colouring instead.

For the ears, use two black cones that have been flattened. Press a smaller pink cone onto each of them. Use a flute vein tool to make a dent and pinch the lower edges together to form ears. Make two holes in the head and insert the ears into them. For the hair, roll two tiny sausages of white and fold them in half. Slightly flatten them at the top and attach them to the head.

To make the hat, lay a piece of black fondant over a black ball of fondant. Shape the centre part of the hat into a nice sphere and use a 2.5 cm cutter to define the hat's outer edge. Attach the hat to the head at an angle.

Method for miniature cakes

You can bake the cakes in specially shaped tins – round, 5 cm diameter tins are widely available for this purpose – but it is much easier to bake large, square sponges and cut out mini-cakes using a round cutter. You can fill and cover these cakes if you wish, but if so, allow them to cool thoroughly in the refrigerator afterwards, otherwise they'll be very tricky to decorate. A large chocolate or vanilla-flavoured butter cake makes the ideal basis for these mini-cakes – it's much firmer and hence much easier to work with, and just as delicious. Butter cake is of course a bit stodgier, so make the mini-cakes slightly smaller than you would if using sponge.

If you want the individual cakes to be very neat, first cover them with plain marzipan. To do so, cut out a circle that fits precisely on top of the cake, then cut off a strip of rolled-out marzipan to the same width as the cake's height and attach this around the cake. Repeat this for all the cakes then allow them to dry a while. Then cover the cakes with fondant as usual, but this time use a very thin layer of fondant to avoid sugar overkill.

You can of course just cover the cakes with fondant and skip the layer of marzipan, but the end result probably won't be quite so neat.

Use a dot of royal icing to wrap the same ribbon around the mini-cakes as you've used on the larger cakes, or attach a strip of fondant if you want to keep everything edible. Cut out circles of fondant in contrasting colours to the fondant you've used to cover the cakes – four different colours give you plenty of options. Glue some edible pearls around the edge of the circle or roll tiny balls of fondant instead. Make a flower as described above for the main cake and stick this on top of the fondant circle.

Tip: Are you planning to make lots of these miniature cakes for the wedding? If so, allow yourself plenty of time because they take longer than you'd think.

Big surprise

Baby shower

And then there it is, the moment that most women would consider to be one of the most special times of their lives – the first time that they're expecting a baby. I've been told that the second and subsequent times are pretty special too, by the way, but seeing as I'm the mother of an only child, I can't speak from personal experience! But one thing I do know is that I remember the day I discovered I was pregnant as if it were yesterday.

We didn't want to know in advance whether we were expecting a boy or a girl; we were happy for it to be a surprise. And we really didn't mind either way, which made it easier I suppose – although the tension built as we approached the day that Mother Nature would reveal what she had in store for us.

Baby showers weren't so common back then and I didn't have one, but they are becoming increasingly popular nowadays. I thought that this unisex design would make a great baby shower cake for parents-to-be who don't know the sex of their unborn baby. And even if they do know, the baby shower guests are usually kept in the dark until the little bundle of joy arrives.

And this cake is of course a great way of celebrating the moment that you share your exciting news with your family and friends, although you might want to make a slightly smaller version in that case. Naturally, this is another milestone that doesn't directly apply to every woman, but I'm certain that it's something that everyone can relate to, and I hope there'll be plenty such joyous occasions among your nearest and dearest.

Tip: If you're making this cake for a baby shower when the prospective parents have already announced whether it will be a boy or a girl, make it all blue or all pink as applicable.

Tip: Has the baby arrived already? If so, simply replace the expectant mother on top with a teddy bear or a larger nappy cake to transform this design into a fabulous 'New baby' cake.

Requirements
Materials
* ✳ round cake drum of 30 cm
* ✳ 3 round filled and covered cakes of 25 cm/20 cm/15 cm
* ⑥ blue/white and pink/white sprinkles
* ⑮ pink dust
* ✳ royal icing
* ✳ Tylose
* ✳ Tylose glue
* ✳ ribbon of your choice

Fondant
* ✳ 1,600 g white
* ✳ 2 shades of pink
* ✳ 2 shades of blue and black

Tools
1. flower blossom plunger size m (PME)
2. star plunger (PME)
3. heart plunger (PME)
4. sugarcraft gun with holed disc and disc with several holes (smallest size)
5. closed scallop serrated crimper 3/4 (PME)
7. scriber needle tool (PME)
8. scallop and comb tool (PME)
9. flute vein tool
10. ball tool (FMM)
11. knife scriber tool (knife) (FMM)
12. brush
13. baby clothes cutter
14. square cutter 4 cm
16. letter cutters

Method

Cover the drum and the cakes with white fondant. Stack the cakes as required and finish off the drum with a nice ribbon.

Washing lines

Knead some Crisco through a piece of black fondant and fill the sugarcraft gun with it. Using the disc with the smallest hole, squeeze out thin strands of black fondant to make the washing lines. Attach four lines to the top cake, five to the middle cake and just one to the bottom cake. Finish off the end of each line with a bow. Cut more black strands into lots of tiny pieces and allow them to dry, then attach them later to the letters and baby clothes as pegs.

To make the baby clothes, use the templates or, if you prefer, you can hunt down some of the special cutters that are available. Soften the clothes' edges by using a crimper to create a crumpled effect or draw on lines, stitching and folds for extra texture. You can have some fun by adding stars, hearts, bows or whatever you like – refer to the photo for inspiration.

Cut out the letters needed for the words 'BOY' and 'GIRL'. Make sure that the letters are all positioned correctly on the cake and then attach the baby clothes.

Nappy cakes

Roll a sausage from 8 g of white. Bend this into a 2 cm high ring. Cut out nine squares of 4 cm x 4 cm. Cut them in half to produce 18 rectangles of 4 cm x 2 cm. To make the nappies, roll up the rectangles. Brush the ring with glue and stick eight nappies around its outside. To make the layer above, use six nappies – glue one in place and stick the other five either side of it. Stick three nappies together to make the top layer. Fix the three layers in place one on top of the other.

Roll out thin strips in two shades of pink to make ribbons for each layer of nappy cake. Finish off with a bow.

Make a little teddy bear head from pale pink. First attach a little ball of dark pink on top of the nappy cake. Then roll a little ball of pale pink, attach two black eyes and a little snout with a tiny black nose. Attach two little ears and then fix the head in place on top of the nappy cake. Make the second nappy cake in the same way, but this time using blue instead of pink.

Biscuits with sprinkles

For the bottom layer of biscuits with sprinkles, I've used iced biscuits – sure to be a popular choice for any little ones present. Turn them so that the icing is face down and spread some royal icing onto the biscuits. Then dip this side into a dish containing the pink or blue sprinkles and allow them to dry.

For the smaller biscuits, cut out circles from very light brown fondant using wavy edge cutters. Dip them in the sprinkles as described above. Use a little royal icing to attach them to the cake.

Cuddly toys

I've attached two cuddly toys to the bottom cake to look like they're holding the washing line.

For the pig's body, roll a sausage from 6 g of pale pink. Cut a third of the way in from both ends. Smooth the sharp edges to make nicely rounded legs. Flatten them slightly at the bottom. Attach the body to the cake with one front leg hanging down.

To make the head, roll a ball from 2 g of pale pink. Make two holes in it for the eyes and insert two little balls of black. Slightly flatten a ball of pale pink for the snout and make two holes for the nostrils before attaching it to the head. Cut a tiny roll of white almost in half to make the eyes. Make two ears from two triangles and attach them to the head. First glue a small ball of dark pink to the body as the neck and then glue the head onto it.

Make the elephant's body in the same way, only this time using light blue. Roll a ball of 2.5 g into a trunk. Make two holes next to the trunk for the eyes and insert two tiny balls of black. Roll two ovals for the ears, flatten them slightly and stick them to the side of the head. First glue a small ball of dark blue to the body as the neck and then glue the head onto it.

Tip: If you think the biscuits make the cake too cluttered, o you don't have time to make the a pretty ribbon around the base each cake is just as attractive. Or if the biscuits are your favourite feature, use them but leave the rest of the cake fairly plain.

Expectant mum

Roll a 20 cm long sausage from 40 g of black fondant, fold it double for the legs and flatten both ends. Make two little cuts halfway along and fold double again to make bended knees, pinching the knees to make them a bit pointier. Make black cones for the shoes, using 1.5 g per foot. Attach them to the bottom of each trouser leg with the toes pointing downwards. You can make lines in them for heels if you wish.

Roll a cone from 30 g of white. Flatten the wide end and stretch the lower edge so that the pullover hangs down over the trousers slightly. Place your finger on the front a third of the way down and roll to make an indentation – this creates a bosom with a tummy sticking out underneath.

Draw a line just below the bosom with some vertical marks as pleats to accentuate the roundness of the tummy. Stick the pullover onto the trousers. Stick a small ball on top for the pullover's turtleneck and insert a cocktail stick.

To make the arms, knead some Tylose through 9 g of white fondant. Make each arm from a sausage of 4.5 g. Make two cuts halfway along each arm and bend them into shape. Make a hole in the sleeves. Stick the arms to the body and allow them to dry well, resting on pieces of sponge for support. If you don't have time to wait, use tiny pieces of spaghetti to fix the arms to the body.

To make the hands, use two flesh-coloured rolls of marzipan, flattened slightly. Slice close to the wrist to create a thumb. Stretch the finger part and flatten again slightly. Make three grooves for the fingers and model the hands into shape. Roll the wrists slightly thinner and stick the hands into the sleeves. In each hand, place a tiny sock made from tiny sausages that have been bent slightly and flattened. Finish off with a bow.

Make the face from 10 g of flesh-coloured marzipan. Gently flatten half the face while rolling to create contours. Use the ball tool to create two eye sockets. Fill them with two tiny balls of white, pressing them nice and flat against the face. Flatten two tiny balls of blue and attach them to the lower half of the eyeballs, then glue on black pupils. Finish off with a dot of white food colouring to add a twinkle. Roll two thin strands of black for the eyelashes and attach them along the top edge of each eye, or you can paint them on if you prefer. Do the same for the eyebrows. Use the scallop tool to create a smiley mouth and make a hole for the nose. Roll a tiny cone for the nose and glue it in the hole. For the ears, use a mini-ball tool to attach two tiny balls against both sides of the head and push them back slightly about a third of the way up. Add dust to create rosy cheeks.

Knead some Crisco through a piece of black fondant and fill the sugarcraft gun with it. Using the disc with lots of tiny holes, squeeze the fondant to make the hair, cutting off small clumps at a time. Attach the clumps to the head, starting at the back of the neck and working upwards until the head is covered.

Tip: If you've used cocktail sticks when modelling, don't forget to tell everyone before they tuck into your cake!

Tip: It's worth practicing with the hair. You can experiment with different hairstyles and give each mum-to-be just the right look.

Baby boy cake

Nine months – how they flew by and yet how they seemed to go on forever...pregnancy is one of the most contradictory times of a woman's life! On the one hand savouring being so at one with the baby inside your tummy, and on the other hand feeling so curious and impatient to see and hold him or her properly. And then, at last, the day of the big event arrives. In my case, I brought a bouncing baby boy into this world. It was time to count tiny fingers and toes. Time to gaze at each other in wonder, time for cuddles. And of course time for cake.

Since I've already made a baby girl cake earlier on in this book, it seemed only fitting to make a cake for a mini-man this time. And what could be better for the new centre of your universe than a cute star-spangled cake with a fabulous floppy bunny on top.

I've chosen to make a modestly sized cake this time – take a look at the quantities, it's smaller than it looks. Needless to say, you can add a larger cake on the bottom to create an extra layer if you're expecting a lot of visitors.

And remember, simply replace the blue with pink, and perhaps make a grey bunny instead of a brown one, and lo and behold you've got an equally cute baby girl cake.

Tip: If you're making this cake for someone else and you'll be giving their new baby a cuddly toy as a gift too, why not make a miniature model of that toy for on top of the cake? Use the method for the bunny as a guideline and keep the toy close at hand – with a bit of imagination and creativity, you can't go wrong!

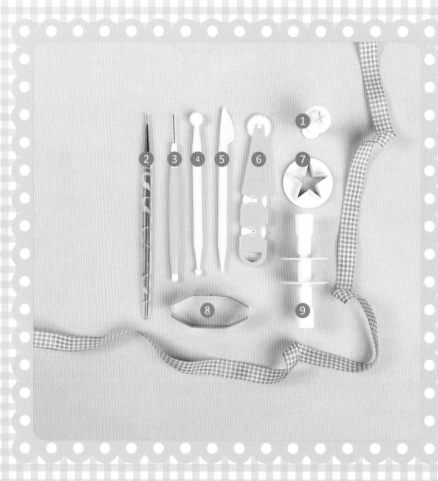

Requirements

Materials

* round cake drum of 20 cm
* 2 round filled and covered cakes of 15 cm and 7.5 cm
* Tylose
* Tylose glue
* ribbon of your choice

Fondant

* 700 g baby blue
* 250 g brown
* white
* medium blue
* black

Tools

1. star plungers (PME)
2. brush
3. scriber needle tool (PME)
4. ball tool (FMM)
5. knife scriber tool (knife) (FMM)
6. design wheeler (PME)
7. star cutter set/3 (PME) scal
8. bow cutter (Städter)
9. multi ribbon cutter (FMM)

Method

Cover the drum with fondant and attach a pretty ribbon all the way round the edge. Using the star plunger, make a pattern of little stars in the fondant covering the outer part of the cake drum. Cover the cakes with light blue fondant and stack the cakes as required.

Bows

Measure the circumference of the bottom cake and divide the number by three to calculate the length needed. Roll out white fondant and use the ribbon cutter to produce three 2 cm wide ribbons of the required length. Use the design wheeler to create the effect of stitches along both edges. Make two lines at both ends of each ribbon and pinch them inwards slightly. Then attach all three ribbons around the edge of the cake.

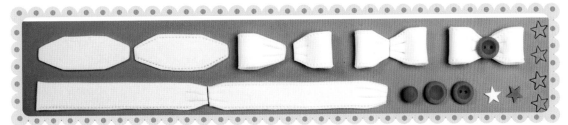

To make the buttons, flatten a ball of medium blue with a ball tool. Carefully use the point of the knife scriber tool to make two holes in each button.

Using the bow cutter, cut out six pieces to make three bows. Use the design wheeler again to create stitches along the edges and fold each piece double to make half of a bow. Attach two bow halves to the cake at each join in the ribbons and attach a button in the centre of each bow to finish off.

Repeat this for the top cake, this time making two bows and two ribbons. Make sure that each layer has a bow at the front.

Cut out large stars from white, medium blue and brown and attach them to the bottom cake. Remember to cut some of the stars in half and place them up against the ribbon. Repeat this with smaller stars for the smaller cake.

Bunny

For the floppy bunny's body, roll a cone from 20 g of brown fondant. Use your knife to draw a line down the length of the body and then make marks crossways to look like stitches.

To make a leg, take 8 g of brown and roll it into the shape of a carrot with rounded ends. Bend the narrow end a third of the way along to make the foot. Pinch gently to create a heel. Make two lines in the point of the foot as toes. Use your knife to draw a line all the way round the outside leg and then make marks crossways as stitches. Stick an oval of white onto the sole of the foot and make stitches in this too. Repeat for the second leg, taking care that both feet are the same size. Flatten the wider, top edges of the legs slightly diagonally and attach them to the underside of the body in the desired pose.

Make each arm from 3 g of brown rolled into a carrot shape. Roll it slightly thinner at the wrist and flatten the hand somewhat. Draw stitches onto the arms too. Stick an oval of white into each palm and bend one hand into a fist. Cut a couple of tiny notches on the inside of the arms to make them easier to bend, giving the bunny a softer look. Attach one arm pointing downwards along the side of the body and wrap the other arm, with the clenched fist, in plastic to prevent it drying out.

Roll a 20 g ball of brown into an egg shape. Draw a line and stitches onto this as well. Make two small holes for the eye sockets and stick two tiny ovals onto them. Add two tiny rolls of black underneath as eyelashes. Roll a cone from 1 g of white and flatten it slightly, then attach it to the face with the narrow end pointing downwards. Make the shape of the mouth using a small ball tool, pressing it downwards slightly to create an oval. Use a knife to draw a seam upwards from the mouth. Make three tiny holes on each side of the mouth as whiskers and attach a tiny blue nose to finish off.

Stick a 1 g ball of blue on top of the body, insert a cocktail stick and then fix and glue the head in place at a slight angle. Then attach the second arm to the body with the fist close to the bunny's eye.

For the ears, roll two strands of 4 g of brown so that they are almost as long as the bunny is tall and flatten them slightly. Halve 1 g of white and roll both halves out into strands, then flatten them and attach them onto the ears, drawing stitches around the edges again. Attach the ears to the head, gluing them to the arms for extra support if you wish. To finish, roll a ball from 2 g of white, draw on some stitches and attach it to the back as a bobtail. Complete the look by making a blue bow.

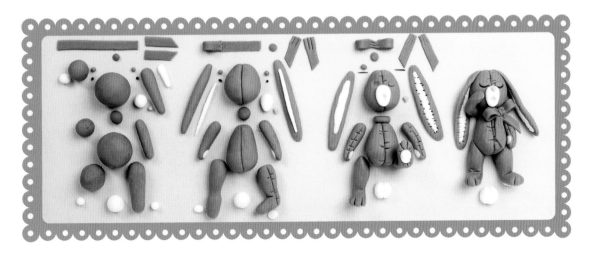

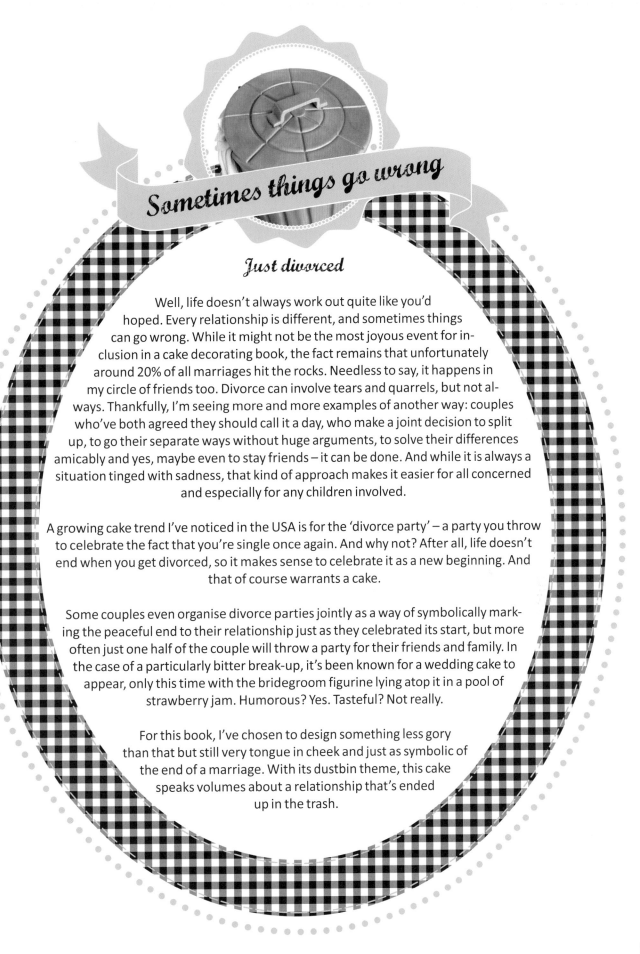

Sometimes things go wrong

Just divorced

Well, life doesn't always work out quite like you'd hoped. Every relationship is different, and sometimes things can go wrong. While it might not be the most joyous event for inclusion in a cake decorating book, the fact remains that unfortunately around 20% of all marriages hit the rocks. Needless to say, it happens in my circle of friends too. Divorce can involve tears and quarrels, but not always. Thankfully, I'm seeing more and more examples of another way: couples who've both agreed they should call it a day, who make a joint decision to split up, to go their separate ways without huge arguments, to solve their differences amicably and yes, maybe even to stay friends – it can be done. And while it is always a situation tinged with sadness, that kind of approach makes it easier for all concerned and especially for any children involved.

A growing cake trend I've noticed in the USA is for the 'divorce party' – a party you throw to celebrate the fact that you're single once again. And why not? After all, life doesn't end when you get divorced, so it makes sense to celebrate it as a new beginning. And that of course warrants a cake.

Some couples even organise divorce parties jointly as a way of symbolically marking the peaceful end to their relationship just as they celebrated its start, but more often just one half of the couple will throw a party for their friends and family. In the case of a particularly bitter break-up, it's been known for a wedding cake to appear, only this time with the bridegroom figurine lying atop it in a pool of strawberry jam. Humorous? Yes. Tasteful? Not really.

For this book, I've chosen to design something less gory than that but still very tongue in cheek and just as symbolic of the end of a marriage. With its dustbin theme, this cake speaks volumes about a relationship that's ended up in the trash.

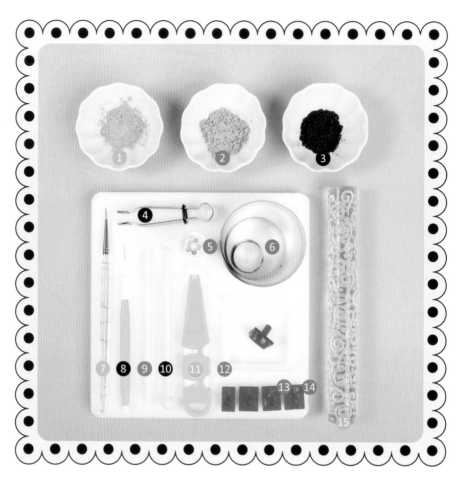

Requirements
Materials
* round cake drum of 27.5 cm
* cake boards of 10 cm and 20 cm
* 2 round cakes of 20 cm
* butter cake 7 cm by 5 cm high
① silver dust or spray
② gold dust
* black dust
③ dark green dust
* Tylose
* Tylose glue
* black ribbon
* ribbon of your choice

Fondant
* 1,000 g grey
* 250 g white
* red
* yellow
* green
* black

Tools
④ closed scallop serrated crimper 3/4 (PME)
⑤ flower blossom plunger large (PME)
⑥ round cutter set (Städter)
⑦ brush
⑧ scriber needle tool (PME)
⑨ knife scriber tool (knife) (FMM)
⑩ ball tool (FMM)
⑪ design wheeler stitches (PME)
⑫ square cutter 6 cm
⑬ alphabet set (Jem)
⑭ strip cutter no. 3 (Jem)
⑮ flower foam pad (PME)
 scallop and comb tool (PME)
 impression roller or impression mat

Method

Cover the drum with grey fondant. Press a 6 cm square cutter into the fondant, repeating all the way round to create the effect of paving stones. Pinch some creases into some of the paving stones so it looks like they have cracked. Dust the joins and cracks with some green and black powder. This makes the paving look more realistic and highlights the pattern. To make the moss, stick some little rolls of green fondant in various joins and create a textured effect using the needle tool.

Dustbin

Take two 20 cm cakes that are about 7 cm in height. Placing one on top of the other, cut them into a tapering shape so that the top is wider than the bottom, then separate them again. Cut a piece of cake cardboard to size and place the top cake on top of it. Roll out some grey fondant and cut a circle from it that fits onto the bottom cake. Cover the top surface of the bottom cake with buttercream and then stick the piece of fondant on top. Then slice both cakes two to three times horizontally using a cake saw. Fill them as you wish, but not too thickly – it's better to fill them three times with a thin layer of filling than twice with a thick one. Insert dowels in the bottom cake. Place the top cake on top of the bottom cake and then crumb-coat the entire stack with buttercream. Once it's been filled, the cake should stand about 17 or 18 cm high.

Roll out a strand of grey fondant and place it around the uppermost edge of the cake to make the stand-up edge. Roll out some grey fondant, not too thinly, and cover the cake with it. Hold a ruler down the side of the cake and run the large ball tool gently along it to create vertical grooves in the fondant. Repeat this all the way round the cake. Since it's an old, battered dustbin, the odd dent here and there will only add to the realism. Attach another strip of fondant over the dustbin's edge. Dust or spray the cake silver grey and then place it off-centre on top of the paving stones on the cake drum.

just divorced

Lid

Brush the 20 cm cake board with Tylose glue and cover it with grey fondant. Leave an edge of about 3 cm of fondant sticking out and cut little triangular notches into it. This makes it easier to fold the edge underneath the cake board so that the underside is partly covered too. Use a ruler to press lines into the lid in a cross shape. Repeat this halfway between each line as shown. Using the round cutter set, press two circles into the fondant, one of 6 cm and one of 11 cm.

To make the lid handle, cut out a strip of 11 cm. Fold 3 cm under at both ends and fold 1.5 cm back again. This makes the handle itself 5 cm long. Leave the handle on its side to dry before you attach it to the lid. Dust or spray the lid and handle with silver grey.

Top hat

Crumb-coat the round butter cake of 7 cm by 5 cm with buttercream and stick it to the 10 cm cake board. Brush the board with Tylose glue and cover the butter cake and the drum neatly with black fondant. Leave an edge of about 2 cm of fondant sticking out and cut little triangular notches into it. This makes it easier to fold the edge underneath the cake board so that the underside is partly covered too. Stick a black ribbon around the hat and then fix the hat onto the drum next to the dustbin.

Bridal veil and tie

To make the bridal veil, roll out a piece of white fondant to measure about 20 cm long by 25 cm wide. Use an impression roller or impression mat to make a pattern of your choice on the top part of the rectangle, leaving the bottom 4 cm smooth. Using the crimper on a little bit of fondant at a time, make a decorative edge along the bottom. Repeat this 4 cm higher along the bottom edge of the pattern. Now decorate the smooth section by making a pattern in it using small cutters – ovals, circles, flowers or whatever you fancy. Gather the veil into folds and drape it over the edge of the dustbin.

Cut a tie out of a piece of fondant using the template on page 134. Just as you did with the veil, drape this playfully over the edge of the dustbin.

Calla lilies

To make calla lilies, you can of course buy special cutters, but a 4 cm square cutter and a 4 cm circular cutter will do the job just as well. Refer to the photo to see how to cut out the petal shape. Roll a strand of yellow and stick it onto the petal. Then roll up the petal, pinching the lower end into a point and bending it slightly. Make four or five calla lilies.

Grass

Roll out strands of green in various shapes and sizes. Flatten them slightly and draw a line down the centre. Bundle several blades of grass together, bending some of them, and then stick a clump of grass up against the dustbin. Marble some grey and white fondant together and make gravel from it, which you can stick around the base of the dustbin too. (For instructions, see the 'retirement cake'.)

Rose petals, rosebuds

Roll out red fondant thinly. Cut out tiny circles and place them on the flower foam mat. Rub the ball tool along the edges to make the petals curl. Stick these on the ground beneath the bouquet as fallen petals.

For the rosebuds, make red cones in various sizes up to 2 g and draw a diagonal line in them. They don't look much on their own but they're very effective as part of a bouquet.

Leaves

Flatten cones of 1 g of green and make lines in them with a knife. Pinch the leaves together at the rounded edge.

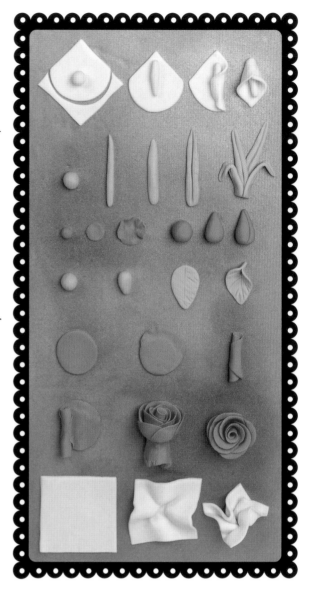

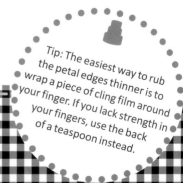

Tip: The easiest way to rub the petal edges thinner is to wrap a piece of cling film around your finger. If you lack strength in your fingers, use the back of a teaspoon instead.

Roses

Roll out red fondant fairly thinly. Cut out as many circles as you can using a 3 cm round cutter. Smooth half of each petal lengthways using your finger. Roll up a petal with the thin part pointing upwards. Roll the next petal around it, but stop halfway along. Then lay the next petal in between and roll until halfway, and so on until you've got the size you require. Make sure you keep the top line straight as you roll.

Once the rose is the right thickness, pinch it together at the base. The petals above will open slightly. Trim or cut away the excess at the base of the rose. Gently rub the petals to open them up a little more. Make about ten roses in various sizes.

Officially, you're supposed to start by folding three petals around the first petal, then five petals and then seven. But seeing as no-one has ever counted the number of petals in my roses and everyone seems to like them anyhow, I'm going to carry on making them based on my gut instinct.

Bouquet

Roll 70 g of green fondant into a cone. Flatten it and drape it over the edge of the dustbin with the point downwards and fix it in place. Attach the calla lilies, leaves, roses and rosebuds onto the bouquet as you wish. Fill any holes using small flowers, which you can make by using the plunger directly on the bouquet and then sticking a ball of yellow in the centre. Then stick the lid on top of the dustbin and fill in any remaining gaps with extra flowers as required.

Tissues

Fill the rest of the space between the dustbin and lid with tissues – because they're an inevitable part of any divorce. To make them, cut out squares of white fondant using either a cutter or a knife. Crumple them up to make them look like discarded tissues.

'Just divorced' and rings

Cut out the black letters for 'just divorced' in a font of your choice. Make the banner from a piece of rolled out white fondant using the template on page 134. If you wish, add stitches along the edges. Stick the letters onto the banner and attach it casually to the drum.

Roll out some yellow fondant, not too thinly. Cut out strips using the strip cutter no. 3. Bend a 9 cm strip into a circle and stick the ends together to form a ring. Bend another strip, this time cm long, into a circle but don't stick the ends together so it looks like the ring is broken. Once they are dry, dust the rings with gold and stick them onto the paving stones.

A well-earned rest

Happy retirement!

When you're caught up in everyday life, the years simply fly by.
You spend your whole life working hard and keeping things
running smoothly for yourself and your family. Before you know it,
the kids have grown up and left home. While it was fun to have
them around, it's also nice when peace and quiet descends
on the house again.

And then the moment arrives when the hard work can stop. It's time to
retire. If you decide to continue working, it's on your terms – there are
no obligations anymore. You have more time to spend with your loved
ones and, above all, more time for yourself.

Retirement is relevant for both men and women, but I've designed this cake for a man who's reached pensionable age because I haven't featured a man's cake in this book so far. And
while not every man will choose to spend his new-found
free time relaxing in a boat, to me this design symbol-
ises what retirement is all about: 'me' time.

Requirements

Materials

* round cake drum of 25 cm
* 1 round filled and covered cake of 20 cm
* Tylose
1 rejuvenator spirit
4 magic sparkle dust (SK)
5 dust in light blue/dark blue/ brown/red
* royal icing
12 silver florist's wire
* Tylose glue
* ribbon

Fondant

* 600 g white
* a little black/grey/green/ orange/flesh-coloured/ brown

Tools

2 oval cutter
3 nozzle tip 12 (Wilton)
6 brush
7 scriber needle tool (PME)
8 small balltool (FMM)
9 ball tool (FMM)
10 knife scriber tool (FMM)
11 strip cutter no. 3 (Jem)

Method

Place the filled and crumb-coated cake onto the cake drum. Stick small rolls of white fondant onto the cake, some on the sides but mostly around the outer edge. Then cover the cake and the drum with white fondant, all in one go. Pinch the bulges in the fondant caused by the rolls underneath into sharp edges and then curl the tops over by rubbing gently to create waves.

Mix light blue powder with rejuvenator spirit and use it to paint the entire cake. Keep it patchy – it might not look very promising at this stage but it creates a realistic effect later. Then paint the cake drum brown. Use a coarse paintbrush to dust magic sparkle dust all over the cake to lend an extra shimmer.

Place some thin royal icing into a piping bag. Pipe a little icing onto the tips of the waves. Use a damp paintbrush to brush it downwards in fine lines for extra effect.

Boat

Knead some Tylose through a piece of white fondant to help the boat dry more quickly and firmly. Trace the boat template from page 135 and cut it out. Roll out a piece of fondant to just over 1 cm in thickness and cut the bottom of the boat from it. Roll out the rest of the white somewhat thinner and use the templates to cut the rear and sides of the boat from it. Allow all the pieces to dry on both sides and then attach them to the thick base. Paint the outside of the boat red.

Stick a roll of fondant in the front point of the boat to reinforce it. Use the strip cutter no. 3 to cut out strips of white fondant. Attach them along the boat's top edges and paint them blue. Cut out a tiny circle using a nozzle and then make a hole in it using a nozzle one size smaller. Make two of these as retainer rings for the oars and paint them blue. After allowing them to dry, stick them onto the boat.

Leave the inside of the boat white and allow it to dry. To make the lifebelt, cut out a white circle using the back of round nozzle no. 12 and then make a hole in it using the front of the nozzle. Paint the lines on the life-belt.

Retired fisherman

Make a cushion from 20 g of white by shaping it into a square and pinching the corners slightly. Stick the cushion into the boat.

Make a 12.5 cm long sausage from 25 g of grey fondant and fold it double as trousers. Flatten both ends of the trouser legs. Make a couple of notches behind the knees and bend the legs slightly. Roll two black cones of 1.5 g each for the shoes and stick them below the trousers. To make the pullover, roll a sausage from 16 g of orange fondant. Make an indentation at one end and pinch around the edges to hollow it out. Attach the pullover over the trousers and then fix into the boat. Model the legs into a natural pose, allowing one leg to hang over the side. Use 1 g to make a turtleneck and attach it to the pullover.

For each arm, roll a sausage from 4 g of orange. Flatten one end and make a hole for the hand. To bend the arms slightly, cut two small notches on one side. For the hands, take two small rolls of flesh-coloured marzipan and flatten them slightly. Pinch to create a thumb just below the wrist. Extend the piece for the fingers and flatten it a bit more. Make three grooves for the fingers and bend the hands into shape. Flatten the wrists slightly by rolling with your finger, and glue the hands into the sleeves.

Make the face using 7 g of flesh-coloured marzipan. Gently flatten half the face while rolling to create contours. No need to make eyes this time. Use the scallop tool to create a mouth and make a hole for the nose. Roll a tiny cone for the nose and glue it in the hole. For the ears, use a mini-ball tool to make two tiny balls, one on each side of the face, and press these back slightly a third of the way up.

To make the cap, slightly flatten a 4 g ball of dark grey. Score some lines onto it and stick a tiny ball in its centre. Cut out a small circle and then cut an edge off it to make the cap's visor.

Cut off the top third of the head, attach the visor and then attach the cap on top of it.

Make some hair, a moustache and a beard from some tiny sausages of grey. Stick them onto the head and use a needle tool to create texture.

Reeds and stones

To make the reeds, glue thin strands of green at various places around the outside of the cake. Attach a little sausage of brown, adding a green tip to some of them. For the leaves, roll strands of green in various sizes. Flatten them slightly and make a line down the centre. Cluster several leaves with the reeds, bending some of them for extra realism. Stick little sausages of light green onto the cake drum at the base of the leaves and use a needle tool to create a grassy texture. Marble together some grey, black and white and use it to make some stones. Attach them to the drum around the base of the cake.

Oars and fishing rod

Make the oars using a little Tylose. To make the paddles, cut out two small ovals and slice off the tip. Make a groove from the top of the curved edge to the centre of the paddle. Roll a thin strand of fondant and stick this into the groove as the handle. Paint the paddle's flat edge red and the rest blue. Stick a strand of white over the join between the two colours. Allow the oars to dry thoroughly before placing them in the rings. Depending on how the oars rest on the cake, you could slice off the paddles' tips at an angle as if they are partially in the water.

To make the fishing rod, roll a thin strand of fondant mixed with some Tylose. Take a piece of silver florist's wire and bend the end at right angles. Insert it into the rod as the fishing line, then bend the rod slightly and paint it brown. Allow it to dry thoroughly before fixing it in the man's hand. Once it is in place, attach a fish to the end of the line.

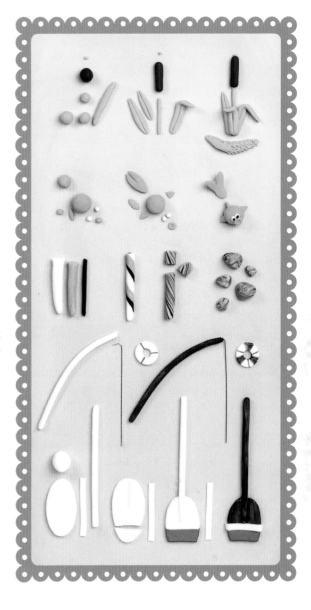

Fish

Make some fish from orange fondant. To make the head, slightly flatten the bottom of a ball. Use a small ball tool to make a small hole in a tiny ball of fondant and attach this as the fish's mouth. Attach two tiny white balls as eyes and then stick on black dots. Roll tiny cones for the fins and attach them to the sides of the fish. Roll a small cone for the tail. Slice it in half from one edge to the centre and ease the two ends of the tail apart, flattening them slightly. Flatten the other end to a point and stick the fish onto the cake.

Finish off the cake with some dots of royal icing as bubbles on the surface of the water. Pipe some royal icing next to the fish, boat and paddles too for extra effect.

Golden wedding

50 year anniversary

As I already mentioned in the 'Divorce' cake chapter, two out of ten marriages end in divorce. But while that may not sound very encouraging at first, it means that eight out of ten marriages do stand the test of time. Fortunately, there are plenty of people who are happy to spend the rest of their lives with their initial choice of partner.

Nevertheless, a golden wedding is a very special occasion. And a celebration of that order most certainly deserves a special cake.

For this special anniversary, I've stuck to a fairly classic design and given it a sense of fun with a couple who, despite having got married 50 years ago, have still managed to squeeze themselves into their original wedding attire...although one of them more successfully than the other. In this case, the bridegroom's waistline seems to have expanded somewhat.

I personally enjoy putting these kind of humorous touches into a cake design because, in my opinion, cake is first and foremost about making people happy. But if you're planning to make this cake for your parents or grandparents and already know that the humour won't be to their taste, you can of course leave the married couple off.

Whatever you do, make sure that the filling inside the cake is to the celebratory couple's taste, because 50 years of marriage warrant a cake that's not only beautiful but is also, and above all, absolutely delicious!

Requirements

Materials

* round cake drum of 30 cm
* 3 round filled and covered cakes of 25 cm/20 cm/15 cm
5 gold dust
8 black food decorating pen
* Tylose
* Tylose glue
* ribbon of your choice

Fondant

* 1,300 g blue
* 600 g white
* light brown
* black

Tools

1 number cutters for 50
2 cherub mould
3 large clover disc and disc with several holes (smallest size)
4 sugarcraft gun
6 stripcutter no. 3 (Jem)
7 brush
9 knife scriber tool (FMM)
10 ball tool (FMM)
11 small balltool (FMM)
12 scriber needle tool (PME)
13 scallop and comb tool (PME)

Method

Cover the drum with white fondant. Cover the cakes with blue fondant. Finish off the drum with a pretty, coordinating ribbon.

Draw a circle 32 cm in diameter on white baking paper. Draw another circle around it, this time 35 cm in diameter, and cut this one out. Fold the circle in half and half again so that you have a triangle. Fold the triangle in half and half again, then cut in a curve from the outer corner to the line beneath. When you unfold the circle, you will then have a flower shape with eight rounded petals. Roll out white fondant and place the flower shape on top of it. Trace around the petals with a needle tool and then remove the flower shape. Smooth over any rough edges with your finger and then place the layer on top of the bottom cake.

Repeat this with smaller sized circles for the other cakes. Stack the smallest cake slightly off-centre to leave room for the married couple at the front. Make sure you leave enough room at the back for the tiny roses.

Tip: Stack the cake in a vertically straight line if you don't use the figurines.

Gold decorations

For the gold rope along the white wavy edges, squeeze out a strand through the small clover disc fitted to the sugarcraft gun. This will produce a ribbed strand that you can twist to look like rope. Slice the rope into sections that are just long enough to fit along one white curve. Brush the pieces of rope with gold dust and then attach them along the wavy edges. Repeat for all three cakes.

Tip: You need literally hundreds of roses to go all the way round all three cakes so you may prefer to use a mould. Or a pearl edging can look just as effective in this design.

Beneath each curve, attach five differently sized small balls one below the other, largest to smallest. To make them, roll a sausage of light brown and slice it into equally sized pieces each of about 1 g. To make the largest balls, flatten one ball slightly. The next size down is half of that, the size afterwards half again, and so on. This will ensure they are all in proportion. Apply gold dust to all the balls before attaching them.

To make the swirls next to them, roll another sausage of light brown and slice this too into equally sized pieces each of about 1 g. Roll them out into thin strands and then curl them into an S shape, curling one end up more than the other. Dust them with gold too and attach them with the thinner end against the balls and the fatter end against the rope above. Use a mould to make the cherubs and then attach them at the highest points as shown.

Make lots of tiny roses by rolling one half of the length of a strip of light brown slightly flatter along one edge, lengthways. By then rolling the strip up in a straight line, the thinner half will remain slightly open to form a flower. Pinch together at the base and trim off the excess with scissors. Dust the roses gold and attach them around the bottom edge of each cake. Set a few roses aside to use in the bridal bouquet.

Bridegroom

Roll an 18 cm sausage from 50 g of black fondant, fold it double for the legs and flatten both ends. Make two little cuts halfway along and fold double again into a sitting position, pinching the knees to make them a bit pointier. Make black cones for the shoes, using 3 g per foot. Attach them to the bottom of each trouser leg. Attach the legs to the cake, supporting them with a piece of sponge.

For the jacket, roll a cone from 50 g of black. Flatten the wide end and stretch the lower edge so that the jacket hangs down over the trousers slightly. Place your finger on the front a third of the way down and roll to make an indentation. This gives the bridegroom a fatter tummy. Cut the jacket open slightly at the front. Make a small triangle impression at the top and make two oval indentations in the front using the flute vein tool. Fill the triangle and the ovals with tiny pieces of white fondant as the shirt that is bulging out from beneath. Score a vertical line for

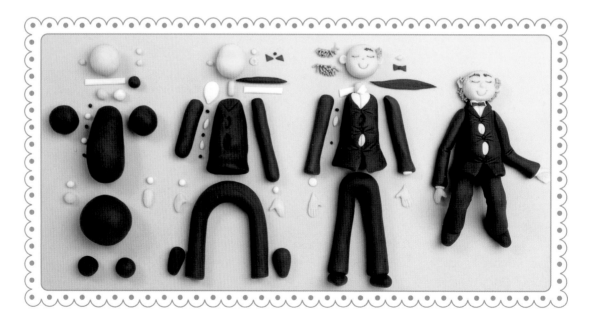

the front of the jacket and do the same on the visible bits of shirt. Make horizontal marks for pleats and then add buttons as if the jacket is straining at its fastenings. Attach the jacket onto the trousers.

Roll a flesh-coloured neck from 1 g of marzipan and attach it onto the jacket. Insert a cocktail stick. For the shirt collar, wrap a thin strip of white around the neck.

Attach a thin strip of black over the edges of the white shirt for the jacket's lapels. Then add two tiny black triangles and a tiny ball for the bow tie.

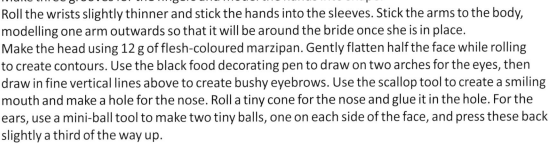

For each arms, roll a sausage from 10 g of black. To bend the arms slightly, cut two small notches on one side. Flatten one end of each arm and attach a small ball of white to each. Make a hole in the sleeves. To make the hands, use two flesh-coloured rolls of marzipan, flattened slightly. Close to the wrist, pinch outwards to create a thumb. Stretch the finger part and flatten again slightly. Make three grooves for the fingers and model the hands into shape. Roll the wrists slightly thinner and stick the hands into the sleeves. Stick the arms to the body, modelling one arm outwards so that it will be around the bride once she is in place.

Make the head using 12 g of flesh-coloured marzipan. Gently flatten half the face while rolling to create contours. Use the black food decorating pen to draw on two arches for the eyes, then draw in fine vertical lines above to create bushy eyebrows. Use the scallop tool to create a smiling mouth and make a hole for the nose. Roll a tiny cone for the nose and glue it in the hole. For the ears, use a mini-ball tool to make two tiny balls, one on each side of the face, and press these back slightly a third of the way up.

Knead some Crisco through a piece of grey fondant and fill the sugarcraft gun with it. Using the disc with lots of tiny holes, squeeze the fondant to make the hair, cutting off small clumps at a time. Attach the clumps to the head, starting at the back of the neck and working upwards towards the ears for the sideburns. Leave the top of the head bald.

Bride

Roll a sausage from 65 g of white fondant. Flatten one end and pinch all the way around to create a wavy edge at the bottom of the dress. Make a few grooves in the skirt to lend the fabric some texture. Cut a couple of tiny notches halfway up the skirt and bend it into a sitting position. Pinch slightly to create the effect of knees. Attach the skirt in place on the cake.

Roll a sausage from 27.5 g of white. Flatten one end and stretch the edge so that the bodice hangs down over the skirt slightly. Place your finger on the front a third of the way down and roll to make an indentation, creating the effect of a bosom, and roll the body thinner below to create a slimmer waist. Drawing a horizontal line just below the bosom and adding some fine vertical lines upwards will make the bosom look fuller. Draw a V-neckline and add some pleats below too. In the space above the V-neck, draw a vertical line with tiny buttons as a respectable button-up neckline. Attach the top to the skirt. Flatten a small ball for the stand-up collar and add a few grooves at the front. Glue it to the body and insert a cocktail stick.

Make each arm from a sausage of 7 g. Make three stripes crossways at each wider end for the puffed shoulders. Cut two small notches halfway along each arm and bend them. Make a hole in the narrow ends of the sleeves. To make the hands, use two flesh-coloured rolls of marzipan, flattened slightly. Close to the wrist, pinch outwards to create a thumb. Stretch the finger part and flatten again slightly. Make three grooves for the fingers and model the hands into shape. Roll the wrists slightly thinner and stick the hands into the sleeves. Stick the arms to the body.

Make the head using 10 g of flesh-coloured marzipan. Gently flatten half the face while rolling to create contours. Use the black food decorating pen to draw on two arches for the eyes, then draw the eyebrows on above. Use the scallop tool to create a smiling mouth and make a hole for the nose. Roll a tiny cone for the nose and glue it in the hole. Dust the cheeks lightly with pink.

Cover the head with glue and use the disc with lots of tiny holes to squeeze grey hair out of the sugarcraft gun. Attach a length of hair around the head so that the sides are covered. Attach two lengths of hair onto the top of the head, curling them back to the rear centre of the head. Squeeze a long strand of hair out of the sugarcraft gun and twist it. Then roll it up into a bun and attach it to the back of the head. To finish off, cluster a few roses in the bride's lap as a bridal bouquet.

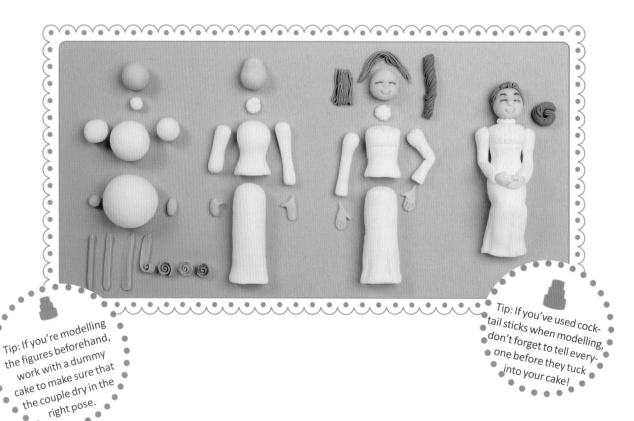

Tip: If you're modelling the figures beforehand, work with a dummy cake to make sure that the couple dry in the right pose.

Tip: If you've used cocktail sticks when modelling, don't forget to tell everyone before they tuck into your cake!

Templates

Baby shower, page 97

Chimney

2x
front &
back

2x
side

Swimming badge, page 55

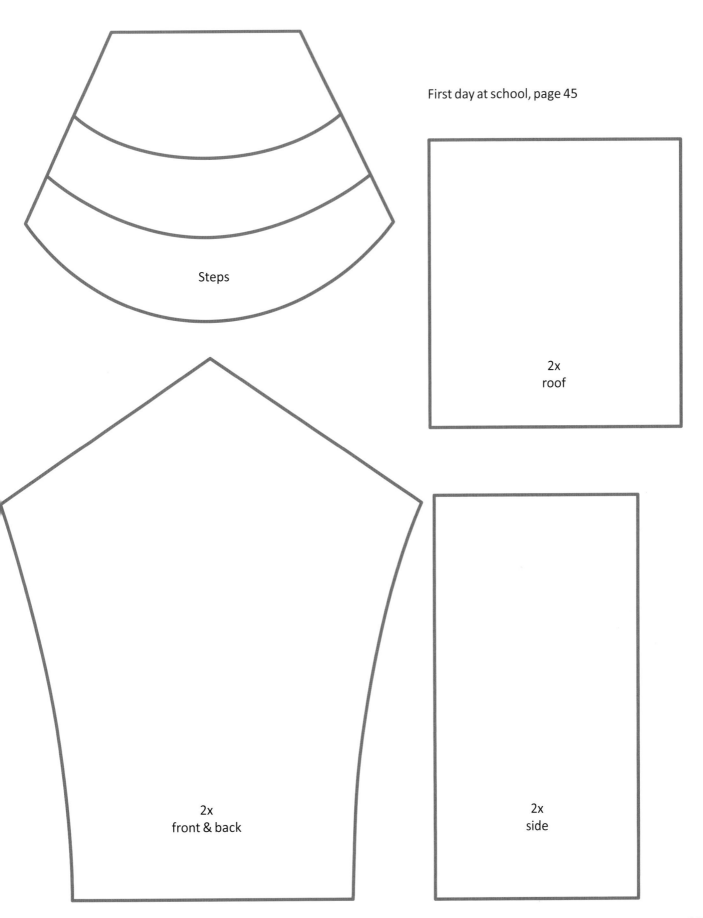

Steps

First day at school, page 45

2x
roof

2x
front & back

2x
side

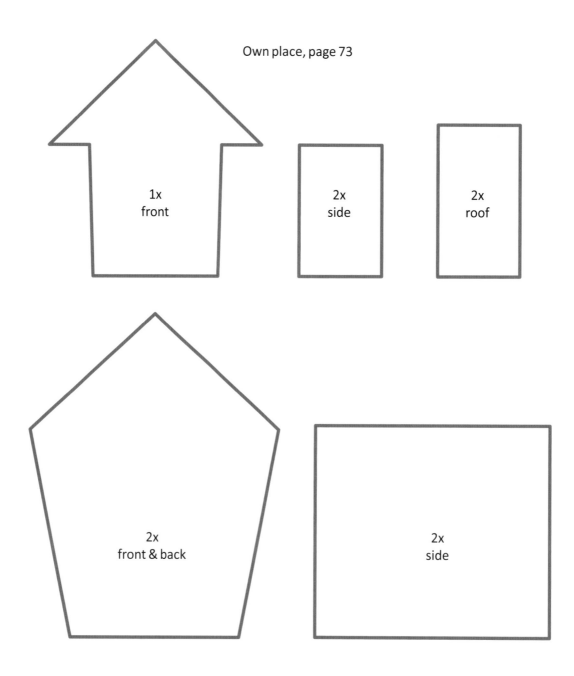

Own place, page 73

1x
front

2x
side

2x
roof

2x
front & back

2x
side

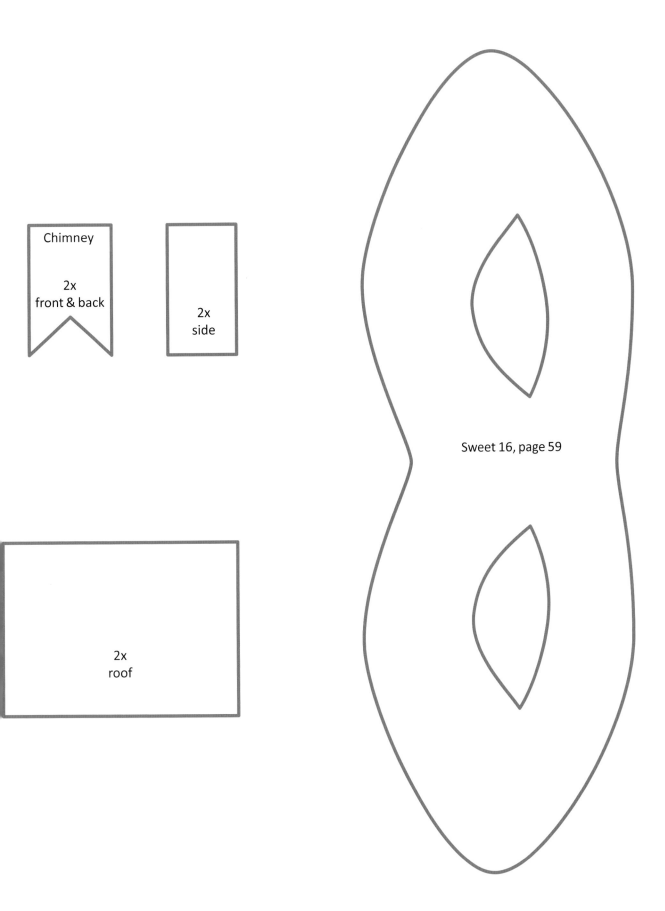

Chimney

2x
front & back

2x
side

2x
roof

Sweet 16, page 59

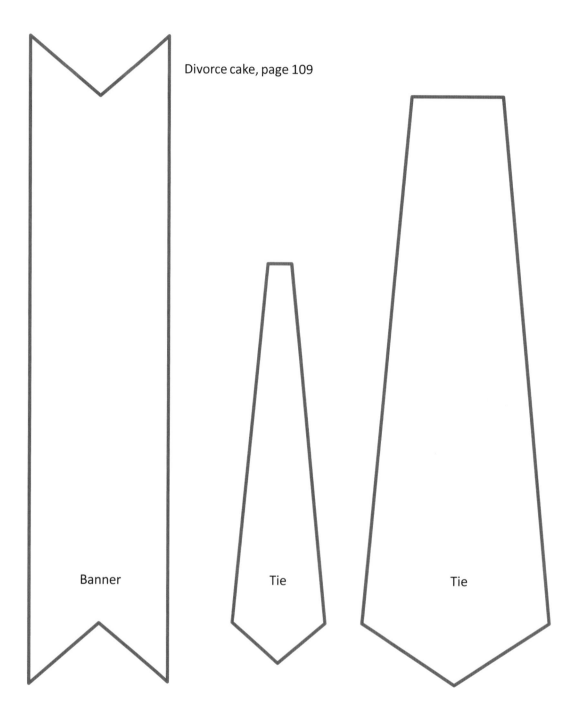

Divorce cake, page 109

Banner

Tie

Tie

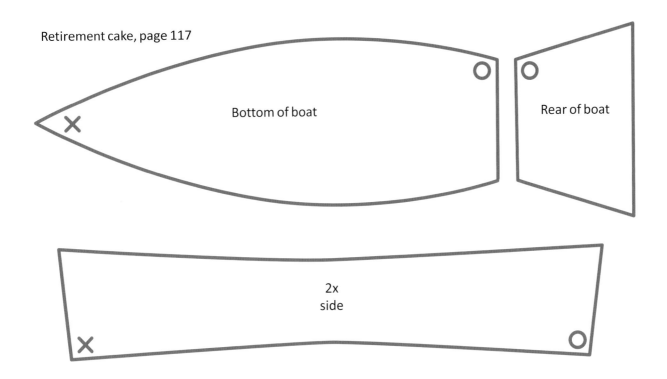

Retirement cake, page 117

Bottom of boat

Rear of boat

2x
side

Thank you!

At the end of writing this, my second book, I once more realise only too well that none of it would have been possible without the help and support of so many people. My name might be on the front cover, but your names are just as important. Once again, I'd like to thank a number of different people.

🎂 Ruud and Liam, my wonderful husband and son. You've both needed even more patience with this book than with the last one. What with the new business premises that we've gained in the meantime and all the workshops, it was a busy period. Not to mention the business trips and trade fairs I'd planned – not particularly well – which took up a lot of extra time. As a result, I had to knuckle down to meet the deadline, which resulted in a wife and mother who didn't have a lot of time left for you. I can only imagine how relieved you both were when I'd finished writing this edition.
Now that this book has hit the shelves, I'm probably already working on my third, but this time I've allowed myself more time to spread the work throughout the year. I hope that this will create more breathing space for all of us. I love you both and I'm very proud of our small but perfectly formed family unit.

🎂 All my friends and family, for your patience and understanding whenever I was yet again too busy to do anything spontaneous. Especially my mother, parents-in-law, Annemiek and Natasja.

🎂 Naturally I also want to thank my wonderful 'cakefriends'. Thank you for the fun weekends, after-parties and for all your Facebook and WhatsApp messages. But above all thanks for being such good friends. And Katja, thanks again for the brainstorm session in B, roomie!

🎂 Lara, I want to thank you again too. Because you once again, over there in Spain, read all my text and changed it where necessary. Despite the fact that it all had to happen at the last minute and I've been such a really terrible friend to you while I've been so busy. Big kiss.

🎂 The girls from the *Mjam taart* magazine. What a shame that I won't be featuring quite so much in your fabulous cake magazine for a while. Thank you for telling me, for my own sake, to stop taking on so much work. I really appreciate the fact that you want me to stay on as a regular part of the team – I would hate to miss out on all the fun we have during the brainstorm sessions.

🎂 Furthermore, I want to thank everyone who's been on my courses and fellow cake-crazy members of the forum, 'Het leukste taartenforum'. And needless to say all of my followers on Facebook and Hyves. It's been so great to see how people have helped and supported me through social media while I've been putting together this book.

Last but not least, I of course want to thank everyone who worked on this book at Uitgeverij Terra Lannoo. Especially Melanie, because you decided that I should write another book after *Een jaar vol taart!*. And Miriam, I hope to be able to work together with you next time too.

Marriët and Simone from House of Origin, thank you for the fabulous design and for styling the photos. Maarten Brunsveld, thank you for taking all the wonderful photos. And thank you also to Ria Brummelman for editing this book.

Sponsors

I've used all sorts of materials in this book, and many of them have been kindly provided by:

www.in2bake.nl: Provided the many kilos of fondant that I used for the designs in this book, both the white and coloured fondant. But check out the website because *In2Bake* does more than just fondant.

www.deleukstetaartenshop.nl: The biggest and best webshop in The Netherlands. Provided most of the materials I've used in this book, but that is just a tiny selection out of its immense range. It supplies literally anything and everything you could ever need for cakes.

www.cakesbybien.nl: The webshop with the best cutters, including the ones from KitBox and the stencils of Designer Stencils. It has also built up quite a reputation in The Netherlands with its own line of Bien cutters, such as the bunting I've used in this book.

Acknowledgements

KitchenAid Nederland: Lent us the wonderful KitchenAid mixers that we used in this book. KitchenAid mixers are built for intensive use and made to last. With an extensive range of accessories/add-ons to choose from, they open up a whole new world of opportunities.

Marna Hairstyling: Michelle, thank you for my fabulous hairstyle in this book. It meant a lot to me that my trusty hair stylist did my hair for me this time.

And thanks also go to:

Vintagewinkel Sugar Sugar
www.sugarsugar.nl

Glas- Spuit en Schildersbedrijf Willems
www.schilderwillems.nl

Hooked on Walls
0800-2352783
www.hookedonwalls.nl

Loods 5
www.loods5.nl

Sources

My own website **www.4theloveofcake.nl** is full of photos of the countless different cakes I've decorated. It also provides details of my cake workshops.

If you're keen to have a go yourself but are just a beginner, or you're looking for more basic information or recipes, take a look at **www.deleukstetaarten.nl** – the website for all you need to know about cakes. Not only the best reviews, step-by-step guides and links but also the best forum in The Netherlands.

Information about the leading Dutch cake magazine can be found at **www.mjamtaart.com**. You can sign up for the regular newsletter, submit photos of your own creations and find endless free downloads of recipes, tips and templates.

Don't miss out on Jozien's cake tips at **www.allesovertaart.nl**. She has collated a whole load of useful links relating to cakes. The site is full of step-by-step instructions, recipes and addresses, so any stores or webshops I've missed out here can be found there for sure.

The handy tables I've used in this book are based on the tables from **www.felicitaartjes.nl**, a wonderfully informative website by Wietske and Annette which is full of tables, handy tips and photos of their most gorgeous creations.

Dutch stockists

Nowadays, there are countless stores and webshops in The Netherlands related to cake decorating, so I've listed just a small selection below.

You can find the names of many more at www.infotaartje.nl.

De leukstetaartenshop
Naaldwijk
Prins Hendrikstraat 31
2671 JG Naaldwijk
www.winkels.deleukstetaartenshop.nl/naaldwijk

De leukstetaartenshop
Ommen
Varsenerstraat 12
7731 DC Ommen
www.winkels.deleukstetaartenshop.nl/ommen

De leukstetaartenshop
Veenendaal
Zandstraat 127
3905 EB Veenendaal
www.winkels.deleukstetaartenshop.nl/veenendaal

De leukstetaartenshop
Wormerveer
Marktstraat 59
1521 DX Wormerveer
www.winkels.deleukstetaartenshop.nl/wormerveer

De leukstetaartenshop
Heemskerk
M. v. Heemskerckstraat 21 A
1961 EB Heemskerk
www.winkels.deleukstetaartenshop.nl/heemskerk

De Taartwinkel
Hinthamereinde 18
5211 PN 's-Hertogenbosch
www.detaartwinkel.nl

Tijd voor Taart
Dorpstraat 33a
6691 AW Gendt
www.tijdvoortaart.nl

Cupcake & Co
Huigbrouwerstraat 24
1811 BJ Alkmaar
www.cupcakeandco.nl

De Bakwinkel
Sintelstraat 31A
6051 BL Maasbracht
www.debakwinkel.nl

Tazzels Taart & zo
Kerklaan 10
2471 AK Zwammerdam
www.tazzels.nl

Love to bake
Akerstraat 126
6445 CT Brunssum
www.love-to-bake.nl

Spullen voor je taart
Damplein 24
3319 HC Dordrecht
www.spullenvoorjetaart.nl
Maak je taart
Kruisstraat 4
1621 EJ Hoorn
www.maakjetaart.nl

Zoet en zo Deventer
Worp 67
7419 Bl Deventer,
www.zoetenzodeventer.nl

Keekies
Hoogstraat 111
5615 PB Eindhoven
www.keekies.nl

Het bonte taartje
St. Janstraat 37
4741 AM Hoeven
www.hetbontetaartje.nl

The Little Cake Shop
Havenstraat 51
1211 KH Hilversum
www.thelittlecakeshop.nl

Sugarlicious
Jan Pieter Heijestraat 117
1054 MD Amsterdam
www.sugarlicious.nl
ACDS
Van der Pekstraat 53
1031 CR Amsterdam
www.acds.nl

Taart en Decoratie Ridderkerk
Amaliastraat 21d
2983 EA Ridderkerk
www.taartendecoratie.nl

Taart en Decoratie
Geldermalsen
Willem de Zwijgerweg 12
4191 WE Geldermalsen
www.taartendecoratie.nl

De Bakzolder
Zuiderzeestraatweg oost 10
8081 LC Elburg
www.bakzolder.nl

Belgian stockists

De Taartenfee
Mechelsesteenweg 252b
2550 Kontich
For stockists, see the website:
www.detaartenfee.be

De Bakboetiek
Keizerstraat 10
2800 Mechelen
www.debakboetiek.be

De Bakboetiek
Rubensstraat 159
2300 Turnhout
www.debakboetiek.be

Coffee & curiosa
Zaffelare dorp 41
9080 Zaffelare
www.coffeeandcuriosa-shop.
be

Het taartenateljee
Dudzeelsesteenweg 391
8380 Brugge
www.taartenateljee.be

Het zoete magazijntje
Nieuwveldstraat 23
Zonhoven België
www.hetzoetemagazijntje.be

Cakes & Stuff
Antwerpsesteenweg 409-1
2500 Lier
www.cakesandstuff.be

Madame Gateau
Houthoek 50A
2430 Vorst
www. madame-gateau.com

Kikkerprins Taarten En Meer
Butsestraat 4
2221 Booischot
www.dekikkerprinstaarten.be

Cakes and gifts
Jodenstraat 20
2270 Herenthout
www.cakesandgifts.be

Taartelicious
Koppelandstraat 77
2200 Herentals
www.taartelicious.be

Cakexclusive
Dorpsweg 10
2390 Oostmalle
www.cakexclusive.be

Yamiemamie Flagshipstore
Brugge St. Michiels
Vogelzangdreef 15
www.yamiemamieshop.be

UK stockists

Almond Art
Unit 15/16
Faraday Close
Gorse Lane Industrial Estate
Clacton-on Sea, Essex
CO14 4TR
www.almondart.com

Design A Cake
31-31 Phoenix Road
Crowther Industrial Estate
Washington
Tyne & Wear
NE38 0AD
www.design-cake.co.uk

Jane Asher Party Cakes
24 Cale Street
London
SW3 3QU
www.jane-asher.co.uk

Squires Shop and School
Squires House
3 Waverley Lane
Farnham, Surrey
GU9 8BB
www.squires-group.co.uk

Webshops

Dutch webshops

www.deleukstetaartenshop.nl
www.cakesbybien.nl
www.spullenvoorjetaart.nl
www.maakjetaart.nl
www.taartendecoratie.nl
www.ellenscreativecakes.nl
www.hetsuikeratelier.nl
www.acds.nl
www.piece-cake.nl

www.bakzolder.nl
www.debakwinkel.nl
www.tazzels.nl
www.aribacakes.nl
www.taartshoppie.nl
www.jetaartshop.nl

Belgian webshops

www.detaartenfee.be
www.dekoekjesfee.be
www.prettysweets.be
www.cakeclub.be
www.cakes&stuff.be
www.taartdecoratie.net
www.yamiemamieshop.be
www.hetzoetemagazijntje.be
www.dekikkerprinstaarten.be

Dutch cake events

I'm delighted that cake decorating has developed into such a popular hobby for so many people that a number of cake-related fairs and events are now being organised regularly, including the following:

www.hollandsugarartshow.nl This cake fair in Hazerswoude-Dorp attracts exhibitors from home and abroad. It is the fair that focuses on gorgeous sugarcraft flowers, where there are numerous live demonstrations and where you can enter into a cake competition of an impressively high standard. Needless to say, I'm in attendance.

www.taartentrends.nl This is <u>the</u> cake fair in The Netherlands. Location: in the middle of the country, see website for details. It is the fair where the cake competition entries have to be real, because once the competition's over, everyone's invited to help eat them up. There are lots of stands from The Netherlands and abroad, and naturally you can enjoy watching demonstrations in all shapes and sizes. At this fair, too, you should find it easy to spot me.

At the time of writing, I know that more fairs are planned, but it's not been confirmed when and where. Cake-related events are becoming increasingly common in Belgium too. The best and quickest source of information about these is undoubtedly **www.deleukstetaarten.nl**.